Defending Yourself Against Cops in Missouri - and Other Strange Places

Dee Wampler

ISBN 1-57921-473-8

Library of Congress Catalog Card Number: 2002104798

Dee Wampler

Dee Wampler & J. Edgar Hoover

"But let justice roll down like waters and righteousness like an ever-flowing stream."
—Amos 5:24

"No man is above the law, and no man is below it; nor need we ask any man's permission when we require him to obey it."
—President Theodore Roosevelt
December 7, 1903

Contents

Preface

"Government is, like a fire, a dangerous servant and a fearful master."
—GEORGE WASHINGTON (1732-1799)

Missouri is the Show-Me State. In our state, police say: "Show me what's in your car. Show me what's in your house."

It probably rarely occurs to you, but every morning you wake up you are protected by the Bill of Rights. At no time in our history have our constitutional rights been more meaningful.

Cops can fly over your backyard and take aerial spy photographs or run a drug dog sniffing around your car on the street or around your luggage at an airport or bus terminal. They can stop you on the highway for little or no reason and demand to search your car and possessions, especially if you fit their idea of a profile. They can knock on your door and accuse you of a crime and once they get their foot in the door, you'll never get them out.

If you're arrested, they can take fingerprints and mug shots and put you in a lineup. For DNA or drug testing, they can snip your hair, take samples of your blood, saliva, urine, and breath or perform skin swabs.

Do you get the point? What the police can do to you and your family is almost limitless.

Only the defense attorney, standing in the courtroom, argues in defense of the Bill of Rights, constantly reminding the judge and jury to remember the protection of our fundamental guarantees.

Fourth Amendment protection against unreasonable searches has been narrowed by drug checkpoints, permitting random stops of autos to search for drunk drivers, sweeps to check for drugs, use of drug courier profiles, drug package profiles, marijuana grower profiles, police good faith exclusions, and "knock and talk."

Fifth Amendment rights are held in disdain by those who think the accused always has a duty to speak.

Sixth Amendment rights are limited by prosecutors and police who hold illegal press conferences and secret grand juries, a tool of the prosecutor who only presents one side of the coin.

Courts are not the only force compressing American rights. Changes in society are pushing the nation toward more restrictions on our freedom. People seem willing to permit police to take shortcuts when conducting searches to unearth criminal evidence.

I sincerely hope your only view of a courtroom is on the evening news. However, should you land in court, this book will cut through the red tape and help you better understand your court experience so that somehow you can make sense of what is happening to you and your life.

DEE WAMPLER

—LAW OFFICES OF
DEE WAMPLER AND JOE PASSANISE
2974 E. Battlefield
Springfield, Missouri 65804

What to Expect from Your Lawyer

"The law and the stage-both are a form of exhibitionism."

—ORSON WELLS (1915-1978)

"The first thing we do, let's kill all the lawyers."

—WILLIAM SHAKESPEARE (1564-1616)
King Henry VI, Part II, Act IV, Scene 2
(Actually a compliment to lawyers,
spoken by anarchists plotting to kill the
king and overthrow the government.)

"Reasonable doubt begins with the payment
of reasonable fee."

Why Don't People Like Us?

There is a nastiness to lawyer jokes that reveals a real hostility. Anti-lawyer attitudes are not new to our culture. Cynical and unfavorable comments about lawyers can be found in the writings of Plato and Cicero and the literature of Renaissance Europe.

Yet many lawyers are known for their enormous achievements and high standards of integrity. They include Sir Thomas More, Abraham

Lincoln, Louis Brandeis, Mahatma Gandhi, and many others.

Lawyers are aware of the endless slurs parading behind their backs. They work long hours to serve others, trying to maintain their integrity in a competitive setting where success is measured by client satisfaction as opposed to justice.

The vast majority of lawyers never see the inside of a courtroom, serving instead as estate planners, corporate wizards, opinion givers, deal makers, and negotiators.

Behind every dubious act of a lawyer there is a client demanding even more aggressive action. Clients hire lawyers to find loopholes around regulations, avoid taxes, gain advantages over others, or simply get them out of trouble while they show little concern for the victim. Lawyers learn to say no to clients, knowing there will be extreme pressure put on them when they do so.

Over the centuries, lawyers have righted many wrongs and instituted social reforms accomplished by litigation. Still, lawyer-bashing continues. Critics claim lawyers have no regard for truth or fairness and will manipulate, distort, or conceal facts to gain an advantage: "You really can't trust a lawyer since they are too clever." They say lawyers are condescending; use legal jargon to intimidate; confuse people about how the law works; are pompous, self-centered, or abusive; are interested only in the dollar; and are not genuinely interested in their client or the legal system. These descriptions apply only to a small percentage of the profession, and with slight modification apply equally to politicians, journalists, business executives, doctors, university professors, accountants, and preachers.

It is not up to an attorney to judge his client; it is up to the judge and jury and if a person is guilty-guilty of what? It's hard to swallow, but the question of guilt or innocence is irrelevant. What matters is what the DA can prove. "If they can't prove their case in court, they ain't got a case."

I didn't coin the phrase, "It is far worse to convict an innocent man than to let ten guilty men go free," but I wish I had. I do not minimize or excuse the terrible cost of crime, the agony and suffering of innocent victims of rape, child abuse, assault, murder, or theft. There is little excuse for most crimes. In our free society, criminals are often free to prey on innocent victims.

This book is not about the victims. Much publicity has been given to, and many books have been written about, the hapless victims of crime. This book is directed to innocent citizens who are charged as criminals, their faces and names plastered across the news media for their neighbors to see—those who are jailed for months prior to trial who cannot afford bail or a good lawyer. This book is about *your* constitutional rights.

Suppose you are arrested and charged with a crime. Your first step is to hire a lawyer. Today's modern lawyer has received a great deal of legal education, but advocacy and courtroom education are still lacking. Many lawyers place little faith in pretrial investigation of their case, or in legal argument in the courtroom.

Every client charged with a crime has a serious problem that needs to be resolved. Does he need treatment for mental problems? Is he being influenced by the wrong kind of friends or coworkers? Did he act under extreme emotional disturbance? Was the act done in self-defense? There may be other reasons for the criminal act (involving family, environment, health, and social status).

Many contest the constitutionality of laws under which they are prosecuted, the rules of evidence, the admission of physical evidence, and the testimony the trial judge allowed. It is these cases, after all, that make new law and further extend and clarify the great constitutional questions that are being answered by judges on a daily basis as our society grows.

Though I personally challenge laws and rules of the court system, I never dispute a jury verdict. It is the nearest thing to perfect justice that mankind has devised. No one has ever claimed it is perfect. You are not entitled to a perfect trial, only a fair one. Jurors make small mistakes during trial, but in the end, the nature and common sense of twelve people will decide your fate.

Behind every crime—of which usually only the bare-boned facts are revealed in the media—there is at least one reason for the accused to justify the act committed. The jury is entitled to know this reasonand judge the facts from both sides of the case, not only as to guilt or innocence, but as to the amount of punishment.

Rule: **If you're guilty or have guilty knowledge of the crime, you may wish to probe for weaknesses in the prosecutor's case, but** eventually plea bargain, taking the best offer your lawyer can negotiate. Discretion is the better part of valor.

Rule: If you are truly innocent, do not consider ever pleading guilty! Plead not guilty, and assert your right to a trial by jury (if the facts are in dispute), or to a trial by the judge without a jury (if the facts are not in dispute but legal questions are in dispute).

Get Going Early

"If you're going to go to war, then let's go to war."
—GENERAL NORMAN
SCHWARZKOPF (1934-)

"You won't always win, but what is important
is to put up a good fight."
—ERNEST HEMINGWAY
(1899-1961)

Once you are arrested or become a suspect, it is important to immediately contact an attorney for legal advice. You should stress to your attorney the need for immediate and quick investigation to get a jump on the case.

You can aid your lawyer by telling him the complete truth, holding back and concealing no facts. Tell him everything!

It is important that he know the bad as well as the good. He can't defend you unless he knows the bad. He may want to file motions to suppress and keep damaging evidence out of court or do investigation to try to minimize harmful facts against you, but he cannot do so unless he knows everything.

Give your lawyer the full names, addresses, places of employment, and telephone numbers of all witnesses, both good and bad, making sure he has the time to immediately contact these witnesses and take tape-recorded statements. It is important to get witnesses committed to a story early–the sooner the better. Tape-recorded statements from witnesses can be taken over the telephone (with their permission) or in person.

Photographs should be taken to make sure the crime scene is preserved. Neighbors and other witnesses should be contacted. Even if they only know hearsay or secondhand information, it is important to contact them because they might provide important leads.

Any lawyer who's too busy or too lazy to make immediate and prompt investigation of your case should be bypassed. Hire another lawyer.

Whenever possible, copies of any available police reports should be immediately obtained by the lawyer and forwarded to you. Most police departments, under the Sunshine Records Law, make the initial police report available, and this report can be helpful to start your investigation.

If your lawyer requests you to perform investigation, do it promptly and in writing. Send him the information as quickly as possible.

If your lawyer is a good lawyer, then he is busy with many other cases. The faster you fulfill his requests, the sooner his attention will be directed to your case and the fresher it will be in his mind. Don't wait until the last minute and don't wait until your case is set for trial. Do the investigation *now*, and work closely with your attorney.

Check the civil or criminal record and any pending court proceedings against hostile witnesses scheduled to testify against you. These are matters of public record at city halls and municipal and county courts, and may provide valuable help in your case.

Pretrial Pleadings

Once you've had a thorough office conference with your lawyer, and he has had time to investigate your case, interview witnesses, and read investigative reports, your attorney will do research on the filing of *pretrial motions*. These take the form of motions to suppress an illegal search and seizure (evidence), or to suppress incriminating statements that you have made (oral or written) in violation of your *Miranda v. Arizona* rights, or motions for protective order (to stop harmful evidence against you from being admitted into evidence). There are countless numbers of pretrial motions.

Many of the motions filed by your lawyer may not be successful.

15

They may be filed for a variety of purposes, which include keeping the prosecutor busy or off base, or using testimony and argument in the motions for "discovery purposes" in order to better learn about the prosecutor's case.

Stay in close contact with your attorney by letter or e-mail to make sure he has all the facts and knows everything that you know to help him prepare pretrial motions. At pretrial hearings, listen carefully, take notes, and help your lawyer.

Selecting Your Lawyer

"A jury is a collection of people banded together to decide who hired the best lawyer."
—WILL ROGERS (1879-1935)

Unless you've ever been charged with a major crime, you can't possibly feel the mental stress placed on you and your family or experience the immediate invasion of your privacy.

You have a quiet peaceful home with loved ones, a job, credit cards, car payments, and the usual monthly bills. You love your family, attend church, and enjoy a small circle of close friends. Then suddenly, your name appears in newspaper headlines and on television, and everyone looks at you in a strange way. You're forced to employ a bail bondsman, select a criminal defense attorney, and establish relationships with people you really cannot afford to hire.

There is the threat of going to jail, paying a large fine, and being a convicted criminal. If you're convicted of a crime, you will lose your job, the right to possess a firearm, and the right to vote–not to mention the embarrassment of it all. Going through this long process is not a pleasant experience.

You lay awake at night thinking what prison will be like and wake up at 2 A.M. in a cold sweat. You're reminded daily of your problems. When you hear about another court case involving someone charged with a crime or when you see a policeman or highway patrolman–you immediately relate to your own problems.

On one hand, you want to hurry and get it over with now so that you can do your time and get on with your life. But on the other hand,

Your attorney should carefully examine each detail.

A good attorney will research the law and file suppression motions.
All pre-trial work is painstakingly done before a jury is even sworn.

Take your attorney's advice. Sometimes you may need to plea
bargain and cooperate with the government.

Your lawyer must be ready for battle,
and prepared to go to the ends of the earth in your defense.

It's a high stakes game with your life on the line. Go to court
with a plan as you lay your life on the line.

Search for loopholes in the evidence.

Your lawyer can unlock the doors to search and seizure
laws that may set you free.

Dee and Joe with F. Lee Bailey.

you think that if you stall and delay the case, your lawyer will call to deliver you with some hoped-for miracle. What should you do? What is the best course of action? Can you trust the judge or jury? Does your lawyer really care about your case? Is he doing a good job? Do you have enough money for a good defense? Where can you go to get the best advice? Your friends give you varying forms of advice, but they don't really know your situation. You don't know who you can trust.

You hope for the best but expect the worst. You place yourself in the hands of a professional attorney and trust his advice. You have faith in the system and put your life in the hands of a jury. However, it is far better to make a good decision at the start so that one attorney handles your case. I can start you on the right path.

If you have a close friend or relative who is an attorney, *do not hire him*. It will ruin a good friendship. You'll do better with and have more confidence in a lawyer who is yours, with whom you can discuss your personal faults, and to whom you can make confessions without embarrassment in a strictly business relationship.

Do not be swayed by television or yellow page ads! Some attorneys advertise because they don't earn enough business by reputation. Just because a lawyer has a law license does not mean he specializes in your problem. Some lawyers are good, some aren't. Some are more knowledgeable than others.

Questions you need to ask yourself include the following:

1. What type of lawyer do I need?
2. Where can I find a good and honest lawyer?
3. How can I choose between several recommended lawyers?
4. Should I tell my lawyer all my dirty secrets?
5. Should I be personally involved in the investigation?
6. How can I keep my legal expenses down?

First, familiarize yourself with the different specialties lawyers practice and realize the vital importance of hiring someone who possesses the correct specialty.

Resist the temptation to employ an attorney because he is cut-rate or specializes in bargain fees. You get what you pay for.

Integrity!

Never compromise on integrity. A dishonest lawyer can cause you endless harm which you may not detect until it is irreparable. A lawyer may mislead you about your chances of winning your case and about the events and developments during the representation. Worst of all, he may put his interests above yours.

Although lawyers are in the business to make money, their business is to serve your interests and protect your rights. Integrity is paramount in your relationship with your lawyer. It is at the top of your list because a lawyer who lacks integrity cannot represent you effectively. In seeking integrity, you should look for evidence of the lawyer's moral behavior, social and professional standing, honesty, and sincerity. Focus on these elements when questioning people who know him (including former clients) and when investigating his reputation with clients who have had experience with him. Look for a lawyer who is praised as an honest, straightforward person.

Specialty and Experience

Look for a lawyer who is *particularly specialized* in cases like yours and who has had experience trying jury cases nearly identical to yours. If you are in need of brain surgery, you go to a brain surgeon–not a general internist. Next, ask him how many brains he has operated on and if he has had any success.

Referrals from Friends and Other Lawyers

With your list of requirements in hand, start calling friends. They are the most accessible source for recommendations of good lawyers, although they may not bring you the best list of names. Stick to your requirements. Try to rely on friends with specific knowledge and personal experience. Seek a *good* lawyer who routinely handles your type of case.

Lawyers are generally knowledgeable about other lawyers' expertise. If you know a lawyer, even if her specialty is completely different from the one you are looking for, she may be a good resource to help you find an attorney in your area.

What's Wrong with Lawyers' Ads?

In TV commercials, all lawyers look the same—respectable and reputable. But their looks are all you know about them. Lawyers advertise because they consider it a client-hunting tool. They advertise because they want business. There is nothing wrong with advertising by professionals, but lawyers' ads fail to provide potential clients with useful information upon which to base their choice of a lawyer.

Concerning lawyers' clientele, about fifty percent comes from former clients, and thirty percent comes from other referrals. Twenty percent is generated by active advertising. The ad attempts to lure you into making an initial phone call or visiting a lawyer's office. A lawyer's ad is a hunting weapon and you are the prey. You are much better off researching and collecting recommendations from relatives, friends, and people you trust.

Interviewing Lawyers

> "Prediction is very hard, especially when
> it's about the future."
> -YOGI BERRA (1925-)
> New York Yankees

The best source of information about an individual lawyer is the lawyer himself. By meeting him and asking the right questions, you can gather all the information you need to select the best lawyer for your case. He should appear truthful in his answers and treat you with the respect and honesty you deserve. If the lawyer hesitates, gives vague responses to clear questions, or patronizes you in any way, you should take that as an indication that any professional relationship with this lawyer will ultimately be difficult.

When calling the lawyer's office, ask to speak with the lawyer himself, explaining that you have a new case you would like to discuss. He should either take your call or return it promptly. Include these points in your initial telephone conversation or office conference:

- Schedule a meeting with the lawyer, and offer to pay for his time at a standard rate. This will establish an attorney/client relationship.
- Ask if he is familiar with any of the parties involved in your case to make certain your conference with him is secret and he does not have a conflict of interest.
- Introduce yourself briefly and present your case, including basic facts, without going into great detail.
- Ask if he has had experience with similar cases and what was their outcome.
- At the initial meeting, evaluate the degree of professionalism that you were able to observe. Were you kept waiting long beyond the scheduled meeting time? Was his office neat and the staff attentive to business?
- Is the lawyer pleasant and friendly–courteous to you, yet professional in every way?
- Is he giving you his undivided attention or does he take telephone calls during your meeting? Your problem is the most important business at hand.
- The lawyer should be a good listener. He should not interrupt you with unnecessary questions.
- Immediately after you have explained your need for legal services, ask his preliminary legal opinion and projections for the outcome of your case.
- The ideal lawyer should be knowledgeable and positive, yet cautious, pointing out strengths and weaknesses. Any lawyer who tells you your case is a *sure win* is either inexperienced or dishonest. No lawyer can predict sure results, especially without further investigation and research.

"People are getting smarter nowadays. They are letting lawyers instead of their conscience be their guides."
—WILL ROGERS (1879-1935)

It's the Money, Stupid!

"I have knowingly defended a number of guilty men. But the
guilty never escape unscathed. My fees are sufficient
punishment for anyone."
—F. LEE BAILEY (1933-)

A pivotal issue is determining how much money you have to pay
for attorney fees and investigation expenses. Lawyers charge based on
their experience and expertise, accumulated over years of courtroom
work and their overhead (secretarial costs, investigators, long distance
telephone charges, postage, photocopies, criminologists, court reporters to take depositions, and other incidentals).

Whether you pay by cash or check, always ask for a receipt and some
form of regular billing indicating when monies are due. Civil attorneys
charge by the hour. Criminal defense attorneys charge by the case.

Can You Fire Your Lawyer Midway?

"If a guy hasn't got any gamble in him, he isn't
worth a crap."
—EVEL KNIEVEL (1938-2007)

Anytime you wish to fire your attorney, you may do so. However,
before you do, consider the consequences. Unless you have a specific
fee contract, letter, or promise from the attorney for a partial refund,
you will not receive a refund.

In addition, the longer an attorney has worked on the case, the
more familiar he will be with it. If your case is near a trial date,
changing lawyers will place you at a distinct disadvantage. Any new
attorney employed will be behind the curve.

The Savvy Client's Toolkit

Your ongoing communication with your lawyer may be oral or
written. It may include various drafts of legal documents. You should

maintain accurate and complete records of the following:

Notes and verbal communication. This file should include notes of all meetings and telephone conversations with your lawyer, your lawyer's staff, and all others regarding the legal matter.

Correspondence with your lawyer. Every letter, fax, message, e-mail message, or memorandum should be filed.

Copies of every document. Some lawyers are possessive of their clients' files–so possessive they sometimes purposely fail to share documents with the client. Make it clear that you wish to receive copies of every document relating to your case, including items from an opposing attorney or the court, memoranda of laws concerning your lawyer's research, or any other documents relevant to your case. This will not only ensure your involvement in the case, but prevent your lawyer from being neglectful.

New developments. You should be made aware of any new case decisions which affect your case, as well as changes in the law. Let your lawyer know what to expect and be kept abreast of any developments that could impact your case.

There are many times when the client does not need to be present in court. Docket calls, reappearances, and other somewhat innocuous, unimportant court dates do not require you to be present, and indeed little is gained by your presence. Often, depositions taken by the attorney will not require you to be present because many times witnesses will feel freer to speak in your absence. This is sufficient as long as you know in advance who is to be deposed and have had an opportunity to provide input and propose questions that you want asked.

Cooperating with Your Attorney

"There's something happening here;
what it is ain't exactly clear."
—STEPHEN STILLS
"For What It's Worth,"
Buffalo Springfield, 1966

"My daddy is a movie actor, and sometimes he plays the good
guy, and sometimes he plays the lawyer."

—MALCOLM FORD
Son of actor Harrison Ford

Once you hire an attorney, *help him*. You have placed your faith in him. Don't work against him; he has your best interests at heart.

- Tell him the truth even if it hurts. Don't lie or mislead him.
- Keep all office appointments and appear promptly. Write out your questions in advance and make sure you understand his answers.
- Notify his secretary immediately of any changes in your address or telephone number.
- Write out comments or suggestions so they become a part of his file.
- If you agree to pay a fee, pay it! The less he worries about your fee, the more time he will have to work on your case.
- You may be emotionally upset and under stress. Do not take it out on your attorney or his secretary. He handles many other cases and cannot handle your stress together with everybody else's. Treat his office staff in a businesslike manner.
- Don't telephone his office unnecessarily. Stop it!
- At court date appearances, appear early, dress conservatively, and wait patiently for your attorney.
- Cooperate and supply any evidence your lawyer requests. If he requests photographs, diagrams, or good character letters, or wants you to attend AA, NA, or some other type of counseling, do it and present written proof to him. Supply him with current names, addresses, and phone numbers of witnesses.

Rule: If you are charged with a criminal offense, whether or not you are guilty, it may mean you need to change your lifestyle by changing your friends, attitude, or daily activities. Judges and juries admire people who try to help themselves. Try to adjust, making the necessary changes to ensure that you never get into trouble again.

Conduct of Your Lawyer

"I am like any other man. All I do is supply a demand."
—AL CAPONE (1899-1947)

"There's no substitute for victory."
—GENERAL DOUGLAS MACARTHUR
(1880-1964)

A lawyer has to be extremely careful that he represents you fairly and honestly within the bounds of the law. He cannot represent you if he has a *conflict of interest* or an *appearance* of a conflict. If any such conflict exists, he should immediately advise you, and you can decide whether you want the lawyer to continue.

Your lawyer will do what he can to present a complete picture of all the events that transpired and to zealously represent you, but in a dignified manner. He will be businesslike and professional with the judge and prosecutor. His conduct is governed by ethics and rules of professional responsibility.

How to Be a Trial Lawyer

"To me, a lawyer is basically the person that knows the rules of the country. We're all throwing the dice, playing the game, moving our pieces around the board, but if there is a problem, the lawyer is the only person who has read the inside top of the box."
—JERRY SEINFELD (1954-)

" You may fool all of the people some of the time; you can even fool some of the people all the time; but you can't fool all of the people all of the time."
—PRESIDENT ABRAHAM LINCOLN
(1809-1865)

Jurors want the truth. They want to know that they haven't been fooled, and that they have been fair and have rendered the best brand of justice possible. Too often clever trial lawyers stand in the way of these goals.

The jury is an intelligent, informed, and wise collective mindset. The average juror is about 40 years old. The twelve jurors will possess among them five hundred years of exquisitely varied life experiences. The worker who scrubs latrines or digs ditches for a living, or who goes home to a cold meal and an empty bed, knows more about the human condition than all of the Ph.D.s one can haul into the courtroom. If you want to know whether you will win your case, ask a barber or a cabdriver. They know what people are thinking.

The most successful trial lawyers are the ones who have the requisite technical skills and have also mastered the highest art of all—the art of truly being themselves in the courtroom. The successful trial lawyers in this country have one thing in common—they totally put themselves into their clients' cases, including a deep sense of caring.

A lawyer must commit to his own self-protection. He will not go to jail for any client, no matter who the client is, or no matter how much his heart aches for the client. He will not give up his license to practice law because he has worked too hard to earn it.

A criminal lawyer needs to use care when he speaks to his client. The client must understand that the lawyer will do all he can within the law allowed for his defense, but no more. The lawyer should say nothing that would be embarrassing if played back later in open court.

A lawyer will try to make good-faith efforts, to choose a professionally responsible path, and to document his efforts.

> "I don't know as I want a lawyer to tell me what I cannot do. I just want him to tell me how to do what I want to do."
> —J. P. MORGAN (1837-1913)

> "I could win all of my cases if it weren't for the clients."
> —HORACE RUMPLOLE

What to Expect at Trial

"Courage is being scared to death-and saddling up anyway."
—JOHN WAYNE (1907-1979)

"Innocent and guilty are harder to separate than Siamese twins."
—CHARLIE CHAN

You enjoy a right to due process and a large number of constitutional rights: to present a defense, to present witnesses on your behalf, to know and understand the state's case and the criminal charges against you in advance of trial, and to fully cross-examine witnesses and present your theory of the case. Few rights are more fundamental.

The Presumption of Innocence

A hallmark of the American criminal justice system is the presumption of innocence afforded every accused person and the necessity that the government prove its case beyond a reasonable doubt.

These majestic phrases—*presumption of innocence* and *beyond a reasonable doubt*—are the two highest values of the criminal justice system. Next are fairness and certainty. Fairness requires no one be compelled to prove his innocence or even produce evidence in his defense; the entire burden is borne by the government. Certainty requires that no person be condemned by criminal conviction without the highest level of confidence that he is guilty.

Aside from these platitudes, get your story and stick with it—and get a good lawyer.

Rule: **Everyone is presumed innocent until proven guilty. An indispensable part of the right to a speedy and public trial and an impartial jury is not to be deprived of life, liberty, or property, without due process of law. Any person ever faced with the awesome power of government is in great jeopardy. It's downright scary.**

What is reasonable doubt? It is based on reason and arises from the lack of evidence. The purpose of a reasonable doubt standard is to communicate to the jury the degree of confidence that society expects of the decision maker in the most serious kind of lawsuit—the criminal trial.

What explains reasonable doubt? As witnesses testify, the judge instructs and the jury listens, only one person is capable of bringing reasonable doubt to life—that person is the defense attorney.

It is a sad fact that every day in some American courtroom a person who is not guilty under facts, or the law, or both, is unjustly convicted. The reasons vary: prejudice, ignorance, mistake, judicial indifference, police ineptitude, deception, overzealous prosecutors, or underzealous defense counsel. Sometimes the presumption of innocence and the requirement of proof-beyond a reasonable doubt are inadequate to prevent a miscarriage of justice.

The Feel of the Courtroom

It is difficult to convey the feel of a courtroom. The very structure is designed to strike terror into the hearts of attorneys, jurors, and observers.

Some courtrooms are very large, about the size of an average American home. Some are small. Many federal courtrooms are so large that communication must be accomplished by microphone. They do not appear user-friendly. The judge sits on an elevated, throne-like desk, on top of and protected by another desk of the same magnitude about five feet in front of the court reporters and clerks. Behind the judge,

33

DEFENDING YOURSELF AGAINST COPS IN MISSOURI

there are permanently affixed symbols or backdrops of the Great Seal of the United States or other figures.

Before I engage in a jury trial in any new courthouse, I always check out the courtroom, sit in the jury box, stand in front of the speaker's podium in front of the jury box, and mentally defeat the intimidation that the courtroom setting conveys. A smart client does the same.

How to Act in the Courtroom

"Where you stand on an issue depends upon where you sit."
—Murphy's Law

I don't panic when I get lost. I just change where I want to go.
—Comedian Rita Rudner, 2002

You are on a stage. The jury watches you carefully for body language, inappropriate behavior, and mannerisms. Never laugh, smirk, or appear to be enjoying yourself. A trial is an unpleasant and serious matter. Everyone, including the jurors, would rather be somewhere else than at the courthouse. From the time you park your car in the courthouse parking lot, you rub elbows with potential jurors. Act polite and look pleasant.

During *voir dire*, (the questioning of prospective jurors) there are many jurors that you may like and others about whom you have no feelings. Make written notes of the jurors you do not like so that you can later make sure your attorney takes them off the jury panel.

During trial testimony, pay close attention and tell your attorney of incorrect answers or inconsistency from the witnesses.

Keep a careful eye toward the jury. Establish eye contact and try to read what the jury is thinking. If the judge overrules your lawyer and makes other rulings, make a list of trial errors so your attorney can put them in his *Motion for New Trial*. If you are convicted, you can assist your lawyer with ideas for the new trial motion since he will not have had an opportunity to read the transcript.

Always testify in your case if you can. It is your life on trial and you are entitled to have a part in the jury decision.

It is better for a jury to see that the attorney is honest and that the client is not trying to hide anything. In the process, the criminal justice system is bettered since it is, after all, an earnest search for the truth. The rewards come in knowing that as the client's representative, the lawyer had a direct part in helping another human being in a unique way.

Much of the success in winning a favorable verdict depends upon selecting a jury that will side with you, the client. Twelve of your peers will listen, weigh all of the evidence presented, and reach a verdict of "guilty" or "not guilty."

Lawyers classify potential jurors into categories to create favorable groups for their cause. Major categories are *leaders, followers, fillers, negotiators,* and *holdouts.* If the attorney is familiar with body language, he can better assess and select prospective jurors and detect subtle attitudinal differences among them—information that may be useful later when trying to convince them to side with his client.

So You Want to Be a Good Witness

"The only joy some people get out of the truth is stretching it."
—Charlie Chan

Best way to get out of a hole is to stop digging.

Keep your answers short, admit necessary things, and try not to explain anything. Remember KISS ("Keep it simple, stupid").

25 Rules to Remember

1. *Know the stage.* As a witness to an accident (or other event), try to visit the scene before trial. Stand on all corners and become familiar with the place. Close your eyes and try to picture the scene, the objects, and the distances.
2. *Learn your role.* Before you testify, visit a courtroom and listen to witnesses. This will make you familiar with court procedures and help you understand what will happen when you give testimony.

3. *Appearance.* Wear clean clothes in court. Dress conservatively. Be pleasant.

4. *No gum, please.* Never chew gum while testifying.

5. *Look like a winner.* Stand upright when taking the oath. Pay attention and say "I do" clearly. When you leave the witness stand after testifying, wear a confident expression, not a downcast one.

6. *Sit up.* Do not swivel your chair or rock back and forth. Put your hands comfortably in front of you.

7. *Don't memorize.* Don't memorize what you are going to say but know your facts so you appear confident.

8. *This is serious business.* Be serious at all times. Avoid laughing and talking about the case in the halls, restrooms, or any other place in the courthouse.

9. *Talk to the court or jury, not at them.* Talk to the members of the jury. Look at them and speak frankly and openly as you would to any friend or neighbor. Do not cover your mouth with your hand. Speak clearly and loudly enough so that the farthest juror can easily hear you.

10. *Listen before you leap.* Listen carefully to the questions asked. No matter how nice the other attorney may seem on cross-examination, he may be trying to hurt you as a witness. Understand the question. Have it repeated if necessary then give a thoughtful, considered answer. Do not offer a snap response without thinking. Do not be rushed into answering.

11. *Explain your answer if necessary.* This is better than a simple "yes" or "no." Give an answer in your own words. If a question cannot be truthfully answered with a "yes" or "no," you have a right to explain the answer.

12. *Don't beat around the bush.* Answer the question directly and simply and then stop. Do not volunteer information not asked.

13. *Correct answers.* If your answer was wrong, correct it immediately.

14. *Answer clearly.* If your answer was not clear, clarify it immediately.

15. *Base answers on what you know, saw, heard.* The court and jury want only facts, not hearsay, conclusions or opinions. You usually cannot testify about what someone else told you.

16. *Give yourself the benefit of the doubt.* Don't say, "That's all of the conversation," or "Nothing else happened." Say instead, "That's all I recall," or "That's all I remember happening." It may be that after some more thought or another question, you will remember something important.

17. *Keep your cool.* Be polite always, even to the other attorney. Above all—this is most important—do not lose your temper. Testifying for a length of time is tiring. It causes fatigue. You will recognize fatigue by certain symptoms: feeling tired, nervous, or angry, or giving careless answers. Lawyers are professional cross-examiners. Don't quibble or argue. You will lose.

18. *Get off your high horse.* Don't be a smart aleck or a cocky witness! This will lose you the respect of the judge and jury.

19. *Tell the truth.* You are sworn to tell the truth. Tell it. Every material truth should be readily admitted, even if not to the advantage of the party for whom you testify. Do not stop to figure out whether your answer will help or hurt your side. Just answer the questions to the best of your memory. Don't exaggerate.

20. *Recall the facts.* Don't try to think back to what you said in a previous statement you made. When a question is asked, visualize what you actually saw and answer from that. The jury thinks a witness is lying if his story seems rehearsed or if he answers several questions in the same terms.

21. *The judge runs the court.* Stop instantly when the judge interrupts you or when the other attorney objects to what you say. Do not try to sneak your answer in.

22. *Don't be wishy-washy—if you know, tell them.* Give positive, definite answers when at all possible. Avoid saying, "I think," "I believe," "in my opinion." If you do not know, say so. Don't make up an answer. You can be positive about the important things that you naturally would remember. If asked about the little details that a person naturally would not remember, it is best to say that you don't remember. But don't let the cross-examiner get you in the trap of answering question after question with "I don't know."

23. *Don't look to your attorney for the answer.* Don't look at your attorney or at the judge for help in answering a question. You

are on your own. If the question is improper, your attorney will object. If the judge then says to answer it, do so.

24. *Don't nod.* Do not grunt or nod your head for a "yes" or "no" answer. Speak out clearly. The court reporter must hear.

25. *Call it the way it was.* If the question is about distances or time and your answer is only an estimate, be sure that you say, "It is my best estimate." Be sure to think about speeds, distances, and intervals of time before testifying, and discuss the matter with your attorney so that your memory is reasonable.

Investigation

"If your investigator is good enough, most any lawyer will do."
—MELVIN BELLI (1907-1996)

Cases are won and lost depending upon which lawyer knows the most about his case.

Copies of the police reports should be obtained as quickly as possible and carefully studied. Witnesses, both pro and con, should be contacted, interviewed, and tape recorded. Photographs should be taken, evidence gathered, and detailed plans made for your upcoming jury trial.

If witnesses will not talk, they can be subpoenaed and a pretrial deposition taken, although this is time-consuming and costly. If witnesses are unfavorable or hostile, they need to be cross-examined in detail and their story investigated. Your attorney needs help to investigate their past, i.e., criminal record, prior marriages, prior court testimony, civil lawsuits, prior drug/alcohol usage, and any reason which may cause the witness to lie.

Obtaining Information on Your Own

Before going to court, you may need to obtain information about another person. Here are a variety of ways:

- Search the Internet.
- The county Recorder of Deeds maintains real estate deeds, loans

liens on personal property (VCC filings), marriage licenses, and other information.

- The Department of Revenue has all traffic convictions (places and dates, detailed driver's license information, photographs, Social Security numbers), and car ownership details.
- The Assessor has descriptions, measurements, and value of land, houses, and personal property.
- The Circuit Clerk has all information on prior or pending civil cases, including depositions and answers to interrogations connected with criminal cases (casenet.com).
- The County Clerk has voter information (which includes voter history) as well as all liquor licenses granted and information about wages of county employees.
- The city health departments and licensing offices will supply a variety of facts.
- Probate Court has information concerning guardianships, incompetent persons, and detailed descriptions and values in estates.
- The Missouri Secretary of State has detailed information on corporations, partnerships, and fictitious registrations.
- The Attorney General's Office has useful literature on many subjects.
- Credit agencies have detailed credit information.
- Ask polite questions of police, deputy sheriffs, elected officials, public employees, and county/city secretaries, and gain a wealth of informal information and advice.
- For small fees, all city, county, and state offices will supply certified copies of important documents which are usually admissible in court.
- Congressmen, state representatives, and state senators will be happy to obtain information for you upon request as part of their constituent service (staff employees are eager to please potential voters).
- Write *federal agencies* and get free information from the Departments of the State, Interior, Energy, Education, Labor, Defense, Commerce, Agriculture, Treasury, Transportation, and Veterans Affairs, as well as the Securities and Exchange Com-

mission, General Services Administration, Environmental Protection Agency, Commission on Civil Rights, Occupational Safety and Health Review Commission, National Science Foundation, Interstate Commerce Commission, and Federal Trade Commission.

- The Government Printing Office in Washington, D.C., has free or inexpensive booklets on a variety of subjects.
- The Fair Credit Reporting Act gives you the right to know what information is distributed about your credit and provides an opportunity to correct errors.
- The Freedom of Information Act (FOIA) is an important-sounding law, but it is sometimes useless in criminal investigations because of the long period of time it takes to obtain responses. Sometimes training manuals and techniques for search and seizure can best be obtained from your senator or congressman.
- Employ a private detective who has confidential sources.
- The official *Manual of the State of Missouri* is a voluminous book listing or picturing every state employee with addresses, wages, nd job title, including photographs and personal history of all the judges.
- High school, college, and public libraries contain massive information, including yearbook collections with photographs and information on students. State statutes and cases are also available.
- City directories list neighbors, employment, and telephone numbers.
- The state Bureau of Vital Statistics keeps death and birth certificates, divorce records, and other facts on millions of persons.
- Check newspaper archives for articles.

An average American leaves a paper trail seven miles long. When you are attempting to locate information about a witness, as many as fifty different records might exist, and only one might lead to the information required to find whatever you need on that person.

You should start with what you know and follow it until you have solved your mystery.

Perjury

If you're thinking of falsely testifying at trial, think twice. You will not succeed in fooling the jury. Perjury in itself is a felony, although it is rarely charged. If a lawyer participates in the telling of a lie, it is subornation of perjury.

What will happen when you tell your lawyer you intend to lie at your trial:

1. Your lawyer will try to convince you otherwise.
2. If you insist, the lawyer is obligated to tell the judge and prosecutor (but not the jury).
3. You will be asked questions in the narrative when you tell your story from the witness stand.
4. Your lawyer should not argue (or develop further) your lies, but should instead argue other defenses.

Rule: **Don't ever lie. Don't ever tell your lawyer you intend to lie when called upon to testify at trial. You can't fool the jury anyway.**

The average American is untruthful several times a day. There is a huge body of scientific research on how the most successful liars get away with it. The art of deception is already the stock in trade for the CIA, the Senate, the military, Madison Avenue, and practically everyone else (including the cops who are interrogating you).

Your Handcuffed Lawyer

"Winning isn't everything. It's the only thing."
—VINCE LOMBARDI (1913-1970)
Coach, Green Bay Packers

There is a bad Missouri case law that prohibits a defense lawyer from commenting at a jury trial on police failure to dust for fingerprints or make other scientific comparisons. This lousy law should be reversed and is a denial of your constitutional rights to present your case in court and attack the prosecution's case. There are many other rules that restrict your lawyer from doing and saying certain things in court.

Sentencing

At your guilty plea, the judge orders a Sentencing Assessment Report (SAR) from the Missouri Office of Probation and Parole. Their reports are more friendly than those issued by a federal court.

You should spend several weeks preparing for this important court date. Supply your lawyer with anything that might be useful to the judge at sentencing, including the following:

1. Proof of successful completion of a drug or alcohol education or treatment program with successful follow-up and aftercare.
2. Drug urinalysis results.
3. Numerous good character letters.
4. Family photographs, including photos of you at work, leisure, church, and in your home.
5. Any awards, certificates, degrees, or diplomas you may have earned.
6. Copies of newspaper articles or proof of previous favorable publicity, achievements, accomplishments, or good works.
7. Proof of completion of voluntary community service.
8. Invite a limited number of well-dressed, well-behaved relatives and friends to attend your sentencing. Give the list to your attorney in advance.

9. Be prepared to answer questions from the judge or make a short speech on your behalf.
10. Consider doing a few days of shock time in jail before sentencing.

At sentencing, the focus is full acceptance/apology by you for your thoughtless, senseless acts that have brought embarrassment and shame to you and your family. The real issue is whether you will succeed on probation *in the future* or whether you will embarrass yourself and the trust the judge placed in you to suspend your sentence.

Accept responsibility and focus on the future. Eat crow big time. Apologize.

Rules of Evidence

"It will be of little avail to the people that the laws are made by men of their own choice if the laws be so voluminous that they cannot be read, or so incoherent that they cannot be understood."
—THE FEDERALISTS PAPERS
(1787-1788)

"If the law supposes that, Mr. Bumble . . . the law is an ass."
—CHARLES DICKENS (1812-1870)
Oliver Twist, 1837

Law Professor: "Every law has its exceptions.
There is nothing on earth that is certain."
Student: "Are you sure?"
Professor: "I am certain."

Jury trials are won by evidence! In a jury trial, there are thousands of possibilities of different pieces of evidence. Jurors are impressed by the energy and impact of evidence; Before walking into the courtroom, think of every conceivable exhibit that might be used to prove your case.

Photographs, satellite photographs, computer re-enactments, videos, slides, diagrams, and any other items of physical evidence are extremely helpful to juries impressed with the imagination and resourcefulness of the attorney. Charts, graphs, PowerPoint presentations, timelines, plaster casts, crime scene reconstructions, models of

44

houses, maps, murder weapons, satellite photographs, and scientific exhibits can be used.

A good attorney assumes from the beginning that his case will be tried before a jury. An abundance of evidence should be gathered and labeled for use at trial. You present your theory of the case in a clear and more understandable manner by the use of physical evidence. A trial exhibit is more difficult to cross-examine than a live witness. In a jury trial, there is no such thing as too much evidence.

Evidence is the means by which the judge or jury are satisfied of the truth of the criminal charges. To be admissible, evidence must be relevant, material, and competent.

Once evidence passes the test of admissibility, it has potential to influence the outcome of the trial. Any piece of evidence, perhaps in combination with another piece, is persuasive to the jury. This is the *impact energy* of an item of evidence.

- *Corroborative evidence* strengthens or confirms other evidence.
- *Prima facie evidence,* if not contradicted, is sufficient on its face value to establish a fact.
- *Direct evidence* proves a fact without any additional presumption.
- *Circumstantial evidence* is a series of facts that, connected by the use of inference, tend to establish the fact at issue. This type of evidence is presented item by item in a chain of circumstance and is coupled with some direct evidence.
- A *presumption* is a deduction that may logically or reasonably be drawn from a fact or group of facts.

Scientific Reliability of Machines

In any type of testimony concerning the operation of a machine, such as a Breathalyzer or radar gun, there must be proof that the machine was in proper working order and had been previously tested for accuracy.

Rule: **An easy way to win a speeding ticket is to challenge the proper working order of the radar gun.**

Videography:

Every law enforcement agency has video cameras. These are used to videotape car stops, arrests, crime scenes, and interrogations/interviews. Oral testimony of the officer is best supplanted with video and audio. The jury now has the ability not only to see but to hear evidence related to the crime in question.

An effective video is one that is planned. Many video cameras have microphones that cannot be disabled. The audio portion of the tape is just as admissible as the video.

Few cops go to the trouble of audio or videotaping an interview. They give a variety of lame excuses or pretend it is against department policy. (It isn't.) They would prefer to testify to what they heard you say rather than have a full, complete, and truthful recording from the start of the interview to the finish.

Films or videotapes of confessions, auto accident scenes, booking procedures, or scenes of a crime are admissible if they are fair and accurate representations, even though they be sensation-creating.

Courts make a clear distinction between communications from a defendant and physical evidence from defendant. *Miranda* warnings need not be given to take physical evidence.

Films are often taken of the accused during the arrest and booking process to show intoxication in drunk driving or manslaughter cases. The accused is required to perform physical tests or illustrate his inability to walk the line, pick up an object, or perform a finger-to-nose test (field sobriety test).

Digital Cameras

Digital cameras capture an image on a disk or memory card. Later the image can be transferred to a computer or printed on a high-quality color printer. There are no negatives with digital cameras.

Computer software allows the manipulation or *morphing* of photographs which can be done in such a way that it is almost impossible to detect. Manipulation of the photos allow for such things as easy enlargements of a particular portion of the photo. It is best to introduce the entire digital photograph before introducing any enlargement from it.

Computer-Generated Graphics

It is possible to computerize re-enactments of crimes or traffic accidents. These re-enactments allow the jury to see a reconstruction of
the events, something formerly left to oral testimony.

To be effective, these re-enactments, or *renderings,* require a reconstruction expert who renders an opinion on the sequence of events
of a particular crime or accident. The expert provides this information to an animator who creates the computer graphics. The process
is very expensive.

Renderings can be powerful evidence but great care must be ex-
ercised to ensure that they match the testimony so the
reconstructionist will portray the scene in an accurate way which
does not mislead the jury. Any deviation can keep this very expensive evidence from being admitted.

Photographs

Anyone having knowledge of a photograph (whether or not physically present when it was taken) can testify that the photograph is
a fair and accurate representation of what it depicts at the time and
place it was taken.

Gory color photos, such as images of a stabbing victim at a morgue,
are gruesome and inflammatory. This does not affect their admissibility as long as the photographs assist the jury to better understand the
case. Missouri allows photos at trial which throw any relevant light
on the case. Unfortunately, there are no laws limiting prosecutors on
the quantity of gruesome pictures so they will load up to prejudice
and incite the passions of the jury.

Diagrams

A scale diagram or map to depict a crime scene will help the jury
better understand locations and distances. The diagram need not be
to actual scale.

Attorneys have their own preferences as to how diagrams should be prepared. They're often made on large sheets of white cardboard clearly showing marked distances to scale, a direction guide and scale guide, the name of the draftsman, and other information. Diagrams are overlaid with clear plastic sheets taped to the cardboard so that witnesses can draw, initial, and date with a marking crayon during their testimony.

Diagrams of scenes have come a long way from the old "bird's-eye view" of looking down. Computer software allows for the creation of three-dimensional diagrams that increase understanding of the scene. With some software packages, a camera can be placed in the scene and moved to different locations thus creating the effect of a movie.

Experiments

"If it does not fit, you must acquit."
—JOHNNIE L. COCKRAN (1937-2005)
California v. O.J. Simpson, 1996
(Commenting on a glove that
did not fit his clients.)

Experiments and demonstrations are admissible in criminal trials. Objections to experiments usually concern the weight given to the experiment, rather than the legal admissibility of such evidence.

- The person making the experiment must be competent to do so.
- Conditions surrounding the experiment must be substantially similar to those at time of occurrence.
- Results must be relevant to an issue in the case.
- The experiment must have been honestly and fairly done.

The Expert Witness

Juries are impressed by the testimony of expert witnesses. Often such testimony can raise the reasonable doubt required for acquittal. An expert possesses superior knowledge respecting a subject about which persons having no particular training are incapable of forming an accurate opinion or of drawing correct conclusions. This expertise can be acquired by study, investigation, observation, practice, or experience.

Opinion testimony is not allowed by nonexpert witnesses since it invades the province of the jury. The duty of a jury is to hear all evidence, including opinion evidence, to weigh it, and decide the issues. An expert witness helps because many conclusions cannot be drawn by inexperienced persons.

Examples of expert testimony include the following:

- *Chemists* testify about DNA results, serology (blood type), semen stains, narcotic tests, effects of drugs upon the human body, nitrate and paraffin tests regarding recent firing of guns, powder patterns, perspiration, saliva, paint chips, glass fragments, metal fragments, hair identification, tool mark comparisons, soil comparisons, and trace metal detections.
- *Physicians* testify regarding force, angle, and depth of stab wounds, force and number of blows by blunt instruments, X-ray readings, physical condition or capability, bite marks, the effects of drugs, mental condition, or sanity.
- *Police experts* testify that crowbars or screwdrivers could have been used to open certain doors or make certain marks. They may also testify about human footprints or similarity of tire tracks.
- *Ballistics experts* testify that bullets could have come from a certain shell casing or were fired from a particular gun.
- *Pathologists* testify about cause and time of death.
- *Dog handlers* testify regarding trained dogs tracking a suspect or sniffing drugs and how the dog reacted.
- *Mechanics* testify as to the condition of brakes and other mechanical matters (based on fallen debris from vehicles).
- *Accident reconstruction experts* testify about the exact point of impact, speed of a vehicle, and braking distance.
- *Graphologists* testify about handwriting comparisons.
- *Fingerprint experts* testify about matching prints.

- *Fire investigators* testify to the incendiary origin of an arson.
- *Dentists* may identify bite marks or teeth.

Rule: **If you can afford the costs, employ an expert witness. Juries are impressed and it will make a difference in your favor.**

Citizen Opinions

Citizen (nonexpert) witnesses can testify to their opinions about the following:

- Insanity
- Intoxication
- The value of property
- Identity of a person
- Speed of an automobile
- Temper of animals
- Recollection of the weather
- Color, weight, light, or darkness
- State of feeling between persons, whether friendly or hostile
- Appearance of a person, whether healthy or sick
- Race to which a person belongs
- Reputation for honesty, truthfulness, law abiding
- That a sound was one of "distress"

The Old Lie Detector Routine

Polygraph tests are not admissible in any criminal case. Lie detector tests have not been proven to have reached the scientific reliability necessary to be legally competent and, therefore, aren't worth a plug nickel.

There is a hidden fear that the lie detector (examiners call it *the instrument*) will replace the jury system, taking the guilt/innocence fact-finding function away from the jury, or that the test will overimpress the jury. Historical notions of due process have always afforded the accused the right to a jury trial by his peers, not by machine. Allowing a scientific test to tell a jury the very thing they are sworn to decide is contrary to our notions of law. Thus, the best lie detector in the world is the jury.

A few courts admit polygraph tests in a perjury case, at a parole violation hearing, or at sentencing.

Rule: **Should you take a lie detector test? The answer is simple— if you have any guilty knowledge whatsoever that you committed the crime, assisted, or helped cover it up, do not take the test. Only if you are one hundred percent innocent, with absolutely no guilty knowledge, should you agree to take it. Don't try to fool the test or con the examiner.**

Polygraph (lie detector) accuracy levels exceed ninety percent. Key factors are as follows:

- The examiner should be trained, at a reputable polygraph school accredited by the American Polygraph Association, in the *numerical analysis method* of chart interpretation. Yearly refresher training is important as an aid to retaining proficiency in recognized standards and procedures.
- It is important that the suspect have food and rest and not be under great emotional stress. Persons who are injured, physically fatigued, or have recently undergone significant emotional shock are not good candidates for examination. It is possible for the suspect to be honestly mistaken about what he believes, and investigators must assess the likelihood that examinees accept their statements as truth.
- Information developed during the investigation is important since erroneous information about the offense, the crime scene, evidence, or the examinee's role in the case could cause the examiner to miss the mark. In a bank robbery investigation, for instance, if a person is found in possession of bait money; it is possible that the person came into the possession of the money through innocent means. A well-qualified examiner will consider asking questions about knowledge of the crime, participating in any way; and connecting evidence instead of just the obvious question, "Did you rob the bank?"

51

- Examination conditions are important. No hint should be made as to the desired results. The polygraph room should be designed to eliminate distractions and outside noises. Once started, the exam should not be interrupted. Any examination that takes place under crisis conditions can get out of control and result in less-than-optimum performance.

Confession During Polygraph Test

The test is a useful tool to help determine whether a victim or witness is telling the truth. It is often used on government witnesses.

Defense attorneys commonly use an initial private, secret polygraph test to see how their client performs.

> Rule: The pretest and post-test interviews are crucial. In the pretest interview, you are asked your life story to get prior crimes off your conscience. After the test, if you are falsely told that you flunked, many suspects immediately confess. These confessions are admissible against you at trial. Take the test if you choose, but once you finish, walk out!

Test questions are always drawn up and agreed upon in advance. There are two types of questions: *relevant* (relating to the crime), e.g., "Did you steal the money?" and *irrelevant* (control questions asked to establish a baseline reading for a normal, truthful response), e.g., "Are you wearing a green shirt?"

Be careful what you say after the polygraph test. Any incriminating statements are admissible against you.

Merely because police may choose to give a polygraph test to one defendant does not mean other defendants have a constitutional right to a test. If the prosecutor agrees to dismiss a criminal charge, it is a pledge of public faith and the prosecutor is required to do so.

> Rule: Don't agree to take a test without help from your lawyer. The questions should be framed carefully so they are not too broad. Don't give in to intimidation by agreeing to take a test.

How to Cheat a Lie Detector Test

A lie detector doesn't catch lies, it checks your reaction to questions designed to make you nervous. It's a psychological billy club to coerce the scared and ignorant.

All of the straps and wires monitor you for erratic breathing patterns, increased blood pressure, and sweaty palms. If you have a reaction to any of the relevant questions but not the control questions, the machine thinks you are lying. If your reaction stays the same, it thinks you are telling the truth.

To trick the machine, you need to artificially raise your blood pressure. When you are asked a control question, tighten your guts like you are preparing for a long prison stay. Then when you are asked a relevant question, relax your body and breathe normally, and the machine will not make a peep.

If you do not think you can pull that off, put a tack in your shoe and step on it during questions. This countermeasure will raise your blood pressure and might throw off the machine. The test will be inconclusive, and you can limp away free.

Voice Stress Test

A hokey device known as a *computer voice stress analyzer* (CVSA) is purported to be a handy, accurate alternative to the traditional polygraph machine. It analyzes tiny vibrations in your voice, captured via a small microphone clipped to your shirt. If you're under stress, your involuntary nervous system causes an inaudible increase in the tremor frequency. The machine can print out results with a graph of peaks and valleys resembling an electrocardiograph. The bottoms of the peaks flatten out and square off when you lie.

When you speak, you send off certain AM and FM waves. But the FM waves disappear when you lie. This is beyond your control.

Results are not admissible in court, although more than six hundred law enforcement agencies now have a CVSA, and many have a new laptop model. They can be used to verify truthfulness from a telephone conversation or tape recording and are much less intrusive and intimidating than lie detector tests.

DEFENDING YOURSELF AGAINST COPS IN MISSOURI

DNA Analysis

In 1953, James Watson and Francis Crick made an exciting genetics discovery in proving that genes are composed of an acid (DNA). The basic information about DNA is familiar to anyone who has read a high school biology text since the 1950s. However, the discovery of the structure of DNA is new.

Human cells contain a nucleus, which, in turn, contains 46 chromosomes that arrange themselves into pairs. Tightly coiled and packaged within these chromosomes are paired DNA strands.

A gene is a segment of DNA that determines physical characteristics such as hair, eye color, and genetic defects. There is a certain quantity of DNA that apparently provides no code for characteristics, and this is referred to as *space* or *junk* DNA. A DNA molecule contains more than three billion units and, although a human receives half of his DNA each from his mother and father, the final links of DNA are unique to each individual.

- Genes are hereditary factors associated with specific traits.
- Genes carry chromosomes.
- Chromosomes consist of DNA and protein.
- Bacterial cells from genes can be transformed into cells that express a different phenotype, and the transforming agent is DNA.

The DNA fingerprinting process employs six steps:

1. *Extraction.* DNA is chemically extracted from a blood sample and purified.
2. *Fragmentation.* The DNA molecule is cut into fragments at a precisely designated point by a restricting enzyme.
3. *Electrophoresis.* The blood or the sample is placed in a gel between two electrically charged poles to determine an orderly pattern of the fragments and parallel lines.
4. *Southern blotting.* The DNA band pattern is then transferred to a nylon membrane (a sheet of heavy blotting paper) and DNA' strands are unzipped from one another.
5. *Hybridization.* Radioactive tagged probes are introduced which

attach themselves onto the nylon membrane.

6. *Autoradiograpy.* The excess probes are washed away and the nylon membrane is placed next to a sheet of X-ray film and exposed for several days, with the end result being a series of dark parallel bands resembling universal bar codes on labels commonly found in retail stores to identify merchandise. The result is an *audograph* or an *autorad*, known as the DNA *fingerprint.*

When blood is taken and matched into a DNA pattern, a serologist can check it against any body fluid found at the crime scene. If a rapist leaves seminal fluid at the scene, he might as well be leaving his Social Security card.

With a series of green blips on a computer screen, the frequency and length of the bars are measured to minute detail. Scientists have used this analysis to determine paternity for many years but police have only recently begun using DNA fingerprinting.

DNA technology is even more precise than fingerprinting or a polygraph. DNA can be extracted from blood, semen, urine, hair roots, or other tissues, and except for identical twins, no two people are known to share the same DNA pattern. Serology can rule out a high percentage of the population for an individual crime and thus free a person who might otherwise have been a suspect.

The actual DNA analysis image, the bar code, can be saved and stored in computers with thousands of others. It is a confusing yet very effective piece of evidence.

Cordless and Cell Telephones

You expect to have the right of privacy when you use wireless, portable, cordless, or cellular telephones, except when police obtain a court-ordered wiretap search warrant to intercept phone calls. You don't. Anyone can listen in on your calls with a scanner.

The Omnibus Crime Control and Safe Streets Act (1968) and the Electronic Communications Privacy Act are federal laws protecting reasonable expectation of privacy against unauthorized interception of wire, oral, or electronic communications.

Congress enacted a law (1994) that eliminated the previous exclusion for cordless telephones and established a $500 fine for intentionally intercepting cordless telephone communications but it is not enforced.

Be careful when you are using a handheld portable telephone or cellular phone. Someone may be listening on a scanner.

Cell phones will yield incriminating evidence. Texting or "sexting" should be avoided, as well as instant messaging.

Domestic Relations Cases

> "The great question, which I have not yet been able to answer, despite my thirty years of research into the feminine soul, is 'What does a woman want?'"
> —OSCAR WILDE (1854-1900)

It is common for distrusting husbands and wives involved in marital disputes and pending divorces to wiretap family or business telephones. Divorce cases sometimes end up with one party being charged with assault, adult abuse, property destruction, or wiretapping. Courts do not allow spouses to tap a phone being maintained in their home unless they are speaking on the phone at the time.

Some spouses will tap and record telephone conversations and simply use the information gained from the call. If the husband agrees to meet his girlfriend at a certain motel, a wife can use this knowledge to hire a private investigator to be present at the appointed time to take photographs which may be used in court.

Talking on the Telephone

The telephone is a wondrous invention, and when used properly, it can save you dollars and hours of time in placing business orders, answering customers' questions, and keeping in touch with family members. The telephone has revolutionized the nation. Cell phones and car telephones are now a virtual necessity.

One should be aware that in criminal prosecutions, the telephone can be a dangerous instrument because police and prosecutors regularly use them to ensnare participants in crimes: .

- Police commonly use informants who pretend to be good friends of yours. They are offered money, plea bargains, dismissal of current cases, or other rewards to enlist their help in telephoning you to record the conversation. Simple recording devices, available at stores in all cities, can be used to record all calls you make or receive. These portable recording devices can be carried, and telephone calls can be recorded at other phones, including pay telephones. The informant will regularly engage you in incriminating conversation, enticing you to admit to past, present, or future criminal activity. Many criminals attempt to talk in "code" by using other names for drugs or stolen property but these incriminating conversations, when taken together with the attendant criminal conduct, will demonstrate a pattern to the jury that your conversation was directly intended to carry out a crime.
- In a *controlled delivery* drug case, the drug transporter is arrested and drugs seized. It is common for police to have the informant telephone the intended recipient of the drugs, making several calls explaining the reason for the delay in delivery.
- The caller will regularly include conversation that directly relates to the day, date, hour, and nature of contraband being discussed so the tape is self-contained or consistent. This will help make sense when played later to the jury.
- Once the tape is recorded, it is preserved and marked for the chain of custody. A typist transcribes the conversation. At trial, the transcript is not admissible into evidence but is passed to the jury to assist them while they are listening to the conversation. The tape is admissible and may be played on a simple portable stereo or an elaborate system where each juror is given a separate pair of headphones.

If you're involved in criminal activity, you should be extremely careful and watch what you say during telephone conversations, especially when dealing with someone you do not trust or suspect may be an informant. Any tape recording made with the permission of one willing participant in the conversation is legal. State and federal wiretap laws prohibit a stranger to the conversation to intercept and divulge your phone call. It is even illegal for you to wire your own business or personal phone and record your spouse, employees, or others who may be using your own telephone.

> Rule: It is a bad idea to talk about criminal activity over the telephone. You run the risk of misplaced trust and faith that someone will tape record the conversation. Learn this lesson now or you may have many years in prison to consider your mistake.

Wiretaps and Bugs

State and federal law enforcement agencies electronically monitor millions of telephone conversations yearly with nearly a thousand bugs and telephone taps. The number of taps in Missouri is increasing drastically as both the sophistication of police officers and knowledge of Missouri's wiretap law increases.

The controversial *roving wiretaps* allow police to monitor targets wherever they go. Undercover agents can plant miniature transmitters everywhere-on a boat hull, in a barn, or at a highway intersection.

Federal authorities notify you that you have been secretly recorded but they do not disclose where you were recorded, why, or what you said.

The cost of a month-long federal wiretap is about $81,000, most of the money paying salaries of police and federal agents who monitor the bugs continuously but turn on the tape recorders only during incriminating conversations. Federal law forbids taping telephone calls that do not concern criminal activity. Electronic surveillance is an important investigative tool, helpful in penetrating the secrecy surrounding organized crime and narcotic rings.

> Rule: Actual wiretapping is rare and difficult to do. You run a much greater risk of having your conversations voluntarily recorded by the other person on the line.

> Rule: If you talk too much, you'll probably say too much.

Best Evidence Rule

Letters, notes, and many other documents may be submitted as evidence. Whenever possible, the *original writing* must be produced in court, not a photocopy. The court must be satisfied that the item offered into evidence is not a fake or forgery. The purpose of the rule is to prevent fraud or mistake when proving the contents of a writing.

Business Records

Thousands of different types of business records may be needed to prove a fact in a trial. Business records are admitted to prove the truth of the matter asserted, notwithstanding the Hearsay Rule Objection. Four things must be proved:

1. The record was made at or near the time of the transaction.
2. The witness made the entry or was responsible for the document.
3. The witness is familiar with how the records are kept.
4. The witness is a proper custodian of the record.

Hospital, police, bank, and many other types of records are admissible. The records must be reliably proved.

A lawyer should be extremely careful because once a business record is received into evidence, the entire document is before the jury. There may be some harmful or derogatory comments in the records that are unfavorable to you and the jury gets all the reports.

Signature Crimes

Prior uncharged misconduct (previous bad acts) of an accused is generally not admissible in court unless it tends to show motive, scheme, design, plan, or absence of mistake. The reason for this law is that the accused is entitled to stand trial for the specific crime for which he is charged and not for some other misconduct he has committed in months or years past.

Example: **If you are charged with rape, child molestation, armed robbery, or another crime where you are wearing nearly identical clothing, or the words used are the same, then the prior acts would have a tendency to suggest that your prior similar bad conduct would be admissible against you to prove that it is more likely that you committed the crime for which you are on trial.**

Offer of Proof

If a lawyer requests permission to mark an exhibit or item of evidence and introduce it to the jury, and if the court refuses, the lawyer can ask for a hearing to make a formal offer of proof.

The lawyer will put the witness on the stand and by definite and specific questions demonstrate the admissibility and relevancy of the evidence. The purpose is to ensure that the judge and opposing lawyer understand what evidence is being offered and why.

Should you later lose the case, that issue is preserved for appeal, and an appellate court may reverse the jury verdict and send the case back for an entirely new trial.

Newly Discovered Evidence

Unbelievably, if you've been illegally convicted, new evidence that might tend to show that another person is guilty and/or that you positively could not have committed the crime is probably not admissible unless it is DNA.

Newly discovered evidence for purposes of postconviction remedies and/or motions for new trial is rarely admitted.

Now that you have a complete understanding of the court system and rules of evidence, you should carefully consider whether you have a defense, and if so, how to convince the jury.

Court Procedures

"In the Halls of Justice, the only justice is in the halls."
—LENNY BRUCE (1926-1966)

[Attorney General John] "Mitchell was arguing strenuously about the law this morning, and I said, 'Goddamn it, forget the law. '"
—PRESIDENT RICHARD M. NIXON
(1913-1994)

Arraignment

One of your first appearances in court should only take a few minutes. This is where the court identifies you as the defendant, the criminal charges are formally read, and the amount of bond is discussed and set.

If you're charged with a felony; your first appearance is not art arraignment. It is only an appearance in Associate Circuit Court for the purpose of arguing bond and deciding whether you want to waive your right to a preliminary hearing. Once bound over to Circuit,Court for trial and/or if you are initially indicted by a grand jury, your first appearance in Circuit Court (or United States District Court) is an arraignment where you are asked to plead either guilty or not guilty.

61

The Criminal Charge

You are entitled to know the nature, substance, and specific conduct of the criminal charges against you. A criminal charge must follow the statute and sufficiently inform you so you can prepare your defense and prevent a retrial on the same charges. Generic (general) charges are not allowed. A definite or precise date and hour are not required but charges about your mental state must be stated (willfully, knowingly, intentionally, negligently).

Amendments or changes in the criminal charge by the prosecution are liberally allowed unless your defense is prejudiced. You should always file a *Motion for Bill of Particulars*, which requests the prosecutor make the charge more specific. In Associate Circuit Court, the charge is a *complaint*. In Circuit Court, it is an *information*. If a grand jury makes the charge, it is an *indictment*.

Suppression Hearings
(the Exclusionary Rule)

Prosecuting Attorney: I ask you, ladies and gentlemen, would a police officer jeopardize his career by lying under oath?

All illegally seized evidence is excluded from court. If evidence is found or confession is obtained after an illegal search, or eyewitness identification is obtained after an illegal lineup, none of the evidence may be used. This is known as the *Fruit of the Poisonous Tree Doctrine*.

You have a reasonable expectation of privacy that your property will be free from intrusion, and society must be prepared to recognize that expectation.

Rules for Pretrial Suppression Hearings

1. *Motions to suppress* raise a collateral issue, independent of guilt or innocence, and normal rules of evidence may not apply. The trial judge hears the evidence without a jury.
2. Motions must be filed in writing in advance of trial. The pros-

ecutor has the burden of proof.
3. The evidence used by the state at trial must be relevant. It must have been seized by police and not a private citizen.
4. If no Motion to Suppress is filed prior to trial, the judge assumes that you have no objection and all later objections are considered waived.
5. You must have a possessory interest or reasonable expectation of privacy in the item you are suppressing (*standing to complain*).
6. If you testify, your testimony cannot be used against you at trial unless you testify differently at trial.
7. Hearsay testimony is admissible to explain the basis for police action.

When a confession is obtained, your lawyer will file a *motion to suppress* alleging that the statement was coerced, that you were not properly advised of *Miranda* rights, or did not make an intelligent waiver of your rights. Physical evidence should be suppressed if there was an illegal arrest or search.

You may lose the argument, but you will invariably learn information at your hearing that will help you at trial.

Voir Dire

"**When you go to court, you are putting your faith into the hands of twelve people who weren't smart enough to get out of jury duty.**"
—BILL COSBY
Comedian

Jurors are uncomfortable, nervous, and confused in this strange new environment. All the time they ask questions like *Do I like him? Can I trust him to tell me the truth? Is he an honest attorney? Is his client guilty?*

The purpose of *voir dire* is to find twelve jurors who are free of feelings, beliefs, and prejudices that might nag them, causing conflict of interest. It is unfortunate when a juror, while deliberating in the jury room, says to his fellow jurors, "My sister was assaulted a few years ago; therefore I'm going to automatically vote for guilty in this case." The client ends up the bigger loser as the result of such jurors' partialities.

Nonverbal behavior, such as facial expression, posture, and gestures, gives clues as to real feelings for anything hidden we might be trying to conceal. We often give ourselves away in the manner in which we cock our heads, avoid another's gaze, or orient our bodies. By correctly interpreting nonverbal cues, you can analyze what is really going on during a trial.

Near where the jury sits (the jury box) is an area that may feel off limits to attorneys. It is important for the attorney to break into this area by walking up to the box, standing as near as he can to the jury, and speaking in a friendly manner. Once a lawyer enters this invisible circle, the jury will better accept him. It is as if every person in the courtroom has an invisible hula hoop around him, and somehow one hoop is not supposed to intersect with another. Once the lawyer causes the hoops to intersect and bump into each other on a friendly basis, he is more acceptable within the jury's social circle.

Scheduled Trials Don't Always Happen

There aren't as many jury trials as you might think. Most civil cases are settled and most criminal defendants plead guilty.

Ten days before a trial is set to begin, the Circuit Clerk sends letters to a number of qualified jurors (usually sixty at a time, or however many the judge in the case requires). Although it takes only twelve people to make up a jury, there must be a large enough group (pool) available to allow both the prosecution and defense to exercise their discretion in picking the jurors who will actually serve (known as making strikes).

State and Federal Courts

"We know that the law is good if we use it properly."
—1 Timothy 1:8

> **"Blessed are they who maintain justice,**
> **who constantly do what is right."**
> —PSALM 106:3

There are three kinds of courts in the United States:
Federal courts are established by the U.S. government. There are fifteen hundred federal court judges and about one million cases are brought each year. Nearly eighty percent are bankruptcy filings and ten percent are minor criminal cases.

State courts are established by a state, a county, or a city within the state. There are almost thirty thousand state court judges who handle over twenty-seven million cases a year, not including traffic and parking violations.

Municipal court is governed by city ordinances.

Once a traffic ticket or summons is received, you make your first appearance. Sometimes a second or third appearance is required when your case is set for trial and plea bargaining occurs.

You are entitled to a trial before the judge or a trial by jury. A conviction will not go on your permanent criminal record since it is merely a violation of a municipal ordinance.

Municipal ordinance convictions or suspended sentences cannot be held against you or used for impeachment purposes at a trial in state or federal court. They can be used, however, in a state or federal *Presentence Investigation Report* to increase your prison sentence.

Associate Circuit Courts

Most prosecutions begin in the Associate Circuit Court of the county that has venue (where the crime occurred). These courts have jurisdiction to try misdemeanors and to hold felony preliminary hearings. Trials are normally before the judge but can also be before a jury.

If a jury has been requested, or once requested and waived, the trial is on the record. It will be tape recorded and any appeal goes directly to the Court of Appeals.

Preliminary Hearings

The preliminary hearing is a critical stage of a criminal proceeding. The purpose is to test the existence of probable cause for filing of felony criminal charges in Circuit Court.

1. You can cross-examine witnesses and see the evidence for later use at trial.
2. You have a meaningful opportunity to defend.
3. A smart move is to tape record the preliminary hearing. The tape can be used to impeach a witness later at trial. The tape cannot be used by the prosecutor if his witness later disappears or becomes unavailable. This is preferable to hiring a court reporter, since an official transcript could be used if the state's witness later becomes unavailable.

If probable cause is found to exist, you are bound over to Circuit Court for arraignment and to stand trial at a later date. If you are not bound over, you are discharged by the judge, but the charge may be later refiled by the prosecuting attorney within the time allowed by the statute of limitations.

Never waive your right to a preliminary hearing unless you are getting something good in return.

Pretrial Discovery (State Court)

Both sides exchange information, reports, physical evidence, and witnesses' statements after the preliminary hearing or grand jury indictment.

The prosecutor is supposed to disclose any information that might reduce the charge, lessen the punishment, or tend to prove your innocence, but rarely does. If he fails to disclose something that might make the trial fundamentally unfair (might have created a reasonable doubt), an appellate court may reverse the conviction and order a new trial (the *Brady* Rule). It rarely does. A criminal trial is a search for the truth, not a mere poker game to be won by the most skilled lawyer. The purpose of pretrial discovery is to minimize surprise.

You have the right to the following:
- Names and addresses of the state's witnesses
- Written statements of witnesses
- Grand jury transcripts
- Reports of scientific tests by experts
- Papers and objects the state intends to use at trial
- Prior criminal convictions of state's witnesses
- Electronic surveillance tapes
- The rap sheet of the accused (the Hoover sheet)
- Psychiatric reports
- The right to scientifically test evidence
- The identity of eyewitness informants

If the prosecutor produces his existing file, that is considered substantial compliance with the discovery rules.

The prosecutor has the right to know the following:
- Reports or statements of your experts
- Names and addresses of defense witnesses
- Papers and objects you may use at trial
- Whether you intend to rely on insanity
- If you intend to rely on an alibi, the names of witnesses and information as to the place you claim to have been at the time of the offense
- Names of all good character witnesses

You must disclose your witnesses, evidence, experts, and details about insanity or alibi defense. If disclosure is not promptly made, the judge may refuse the evidence.

Either attorney may interview the other party's witnesses without the consent of the other attorney. A witness has the right to refuse to talk with either attorney, but this may be mentioned at trial.

Rule: **If you are expecting to be a witness in an upcoming court testimony, don't discuss the case with anyone outside the courtroom. Do all your talking inside the courtroom.**

Media Publicity

"All I know is just what I read in the papers."
—WILL ROGERS (1878-1935)

"One of TV's great contributions is that it brought murder back into the home, where it belongs."
—ALFRED HITCHCOCK (1899-1980)

Prosecutors and police can demoralize you by talking about you to the media. It makes life hell, embarrasses your family, and ostracizes you from the community. The prosecutor speaks through press releases, announcing indictments and long, rambling criminal charges, describing legal motions (a way of getting facts into the media that are not admissible in court), and bail and pretrial detention hearings.

> Rule: **It is difficult to represent a demoralized person. Prosecutors want you to surrender, quickly plead guilty, and snitch on your friends.**

It is important that the news media have access to nonprejudicial information about a crime. The press needs police cooperation to accurately and fairly report the occurrence of a crime while giving facts to the public. Such facts include the following:

1. Information necessary to aid in the suspect's apprehension
2. A warning to the public of any dangers that an at-large suspect might present
3. Name, age, residence, occupation, and family status of those arrested

Lawyers are careful about what they say outside the courtroom prior to trial. Ethical rules prohibit attorneys from making statements to the press that are intended to influence the public.

Few prosecutors understand that they are to make every effort to convince police not to make prejudicial statements about the accused

68

Some prosecutors and police shoot their mouths off and poison public opinion against you. Any prosecutor's statement to the media is required to conclude with "The accused is presumed innocent." This law is seldom obeyed, and you have no recourse.

The fact is, you are going to be a news story for the next twenty-four hours. Get used to it. If you don't like it, don't read the newspaper or watch TV.

Change of Judge (Know thy Judge)

"I don't want to know what the law is, I want to know
who the judge is."
—Roy M. Cohn
Famous criminal lawyer, 1988

'Judges, like Caesar's wife, should be above suspicion."
—Charles Bowen
English jurist, 1889

"I request a change of venue to Virginia. No wait ... Texas."

A word needs to be said about judges. They are honest and they are hardworking.

Every judge has an individual personality and, therefore, has a tendency to lean in certain directions. It is up to your lawyer to acquaint you with the judge's track record. Then you make the call.

Within a reasonable period of time after charges are filed, you may ask the court for a change of venue to another location or request that the judge step aside and disqualify himself.

In federal court, the motions are rarely successful. In state court, you can disqualify the associate judge before the preliminary hearing, and within ten days after Circuit Court arraignment, you can disqualify the circuit judge and/or request a change of venue. Your case will go to an adjacent county unless publicity has damaged your reputation so that you believe your case should be moved a greater distance.

Judges will disqualify themselves on their own motion if their impartiality can be questioned by a reasonable man.

Conduct of Trial

"Three things belong to the judge: to hear courteously, to answer wisely, and to decide impartially."
—SOCRATES (469-399 B.C.)

"Judge: Are you trying to show contempt for the court?
Flower Belle Lee: No, your honor, I'm doing my best to hide it."
—ADDISON RICHARDS (1887-1964)
AND—MAE WEST (1892-1980)
My Little Chickadee (1940)

It is the duty of the trial judge to maintain dignity, order, and decorum in the courtroom. Although the judge normally leaves questioning to the attorneys, he has the power to question a witness and will do so to clear up any misconceptions. He exercises judicial self-restraint, and may not indicate his belief of guilt or innocence nor comment on the evidence.

The court, at its discretion, may exclude trial witnesses from the courtroom except when they are testifying. This ensures that their testimony will not be influenced by what they have heard in the courtroom.

Rule: The judge is always to appear neutral and show no favoritism toward either side. The best judge is one who listens to both arguments and decides the case strictly according to law.

"Trust one another (but brand your cattle)."
—CLARENCE DARROW (1857-1938)

The Opening Statement

"Unless you speak intelligible words with your tongue,
how will anyone know what you are saying?
You will just be speaking into the air."
—1 CORINTHIANS 14:9

"Hollow words, I deem, are the words of ills."
—AESCHYLUS (525-456 B.C.)

"Be always sure you are right-then go ahead."
—DAVY CROCKETT (1786-1836)

The opening statement does not entitle lawyers to argue their case, but merely to preview for the jury what the attorney believes the evidence will be. It helps make the case easier for the jury to understand.

The prosecutor must give an opening statement and outline his evidence. The defense attorney need not make an opening statement, but makes a serious mistake by not doing so. In the vast majority of the cases when an opening statement is not given by a defense attorney, the client ends up being convicted. Notwithstanding each juror's answer during *voir dire,* surveys show that jurors do hold it against the accused if he does not testify or present evidence to explain his side of the case.

The opening is an outline of expected evidence. Argument is not allowed. Talking to the jury in the opening statement is an opportunity by expression, gesture, and mannerism to present your side of the case.

The prosecution will make reference to the victim in an attempt to get sympathy and prejudice. The defense counsel will use his client's first name, tell the jury good things about his case, and touch his client's shoulder to humanize him.

Rule: Jurors tend to form opinions about the case early in the opening statement. The vast majority, more than seventy-five percent of those opinions, are never changed during a trial.

By the end of the opening statements, most jury members have made a tentative decision as to how they are leaning without hearing one drop of evidence. The defense attorney should get his theory in early so the jury can be considering his side of the case.

Impeachment by Prior Convictions and Bad Conduct

That's my story and I'm sticking with it.

A witness may be cross-examined and *impeached* by a prior misdemeanor or felony conviction. There is an absolute right to ask such questions, no matter how old or remote the crime, except that federal court limits prior convictions only to felonies within the preceding ten years.

Evidence may be shown that on a prior occasion the accused committed acts that constitute a crime (even though he may not have been actually charged and convicted). Admittedly, evidence of prior bad acts may be prejudicial and inflame the passions of a jury; however, it is admissible and helps to establish motive, intent, and absence of accident or mistake.

The prosecutor cannot call a witness to testify who is expected to take the Fifth Amendment but the defense attorney may. If a deposition or prior sworn testimony is available, and if the witness is otherwise unavailable to attend trial, his prior testimony may be read to the jury.

Once a witness is asked about prior inconsistent statements, his credibility can then be bolstered by asking about prior consistent statements. Any evidence to bolster a witness is admissible if offered in rebuttal.

If a witness is asked whether the accused has ever been in trouble or arrested, the door is opened for specifics about prior arrests and confrontations with police, regardless of whether a conviction followed. Only a fool would ask such a question on his client's behalf.

Witnesses may be cross-examined as to any matters within the fair purview of direct examination, and otherwise inadmissible evidence may come to light if the witness opens the door. Wide latitude is given to show bias, motive, ill feeling, prejudice, or interest on the part of any witness.

Rule: **If you take the witness stand, be prepared to answer embarrassing questions.**

Good Character Witnesses

The law presumes that a person of good character would be less likely to commit a crime than one of bad character. Therefore, evidence of the good character of the defendant by witnesses who are familiar with his reputation in the community for truthfulness, honesty, good morals, and being a law-abiding citizen, is admissible.

A witness may be shown to be a good friend of the accused or asked about other aspects of the accused's character, such as prior arrests that did not result in convictions. Thus, a good character witness can hurt a defendant.

Rule: **If you are on trial, think twice before presenting good character witnesses. You open the door to possible embarrassing evidence, prior arrests, or bad acts. Present good character evidence only if you are squeaky clean.**

Eyewitness Identification

One of the best types of proof is eyewitness identification. Factors considered by the court in determining the reliability of the identification include the following:

- The opportunity to view the criminal at the time of the crime
- The witness' degree of attention
- The accuracy of the prior description of the accused
- The level of certainty demonstrated by the witness at the confrontation
- Length of time between the crime and confrontation

Privileges

For many years, the law has recognized certain conversations to be private and secret. Proof of what was said at these conversations cannot ever be admitted into evidence. Once it is shown that a witness is getting ready to answer a question using privileged information, an appropriate objection is made and the judge will forbid an answer.

Attorney-Client Privilege

Any conversation between an attorney and a' client is secret. The client asserts the privilege and can prohibit his lawyer from ever testifying against him. Anytime a lawyer is asked questions about what a client has said, the lawyer will refuse to answer. If the communication was made confidentially to the attorney to 'obtain legal advice, it is forever secret.

If third persons are present and there is no proof that the conversation was intended to be private, the privilege is deemed waived. When you meet with your lawyer, do not take friends or relatives you do not trust.

The only exceptions are the *fraud exception,* where the attorney actually becomes involved in a crime with a client, and the *tax reporting exception* (information given to your lawyer in preparing a tax return is not privileged).

Husband-Wife Privilege

Neither spouse may testify against the other as long as they are legally married. This privilege may be invoked only by the witness spouse.

The confidential conversation survives death or divorce if the communication was intended to be confidential. The purpose is to preserve families by preventing spouses from becoming adversaries against one another in criminal proceedings. Exceptions are as follows:

- Where spouses are joint participants in a crime
- Where the crime occurred before the marriage

- Where spouses are involved in a divorce case
- Where the crime was child molestation or wife beating

Physician-Patient Privilege

Conversations between you and your doctor are secret. The purpose is to protect you so you may admit to illnesses to receive medical treatment and so the doctor may ask about your medical problems to properly treat you.

The Health Insurance Portability and Accountability Act (HIPAA) attempts to maintain privacy without compromising health care. The law provides national standards to protect individuals' medical records and personal health information, sets boundaries for the use and release of the records, and holds violators accountable with civil and criminal penalties.

The law will have little or no useful effect and still does not stop hospitals from allowing police into emergency rooms so they can question suspects while being given emergency medical treatment and/or eavesdrop on you while you talk to your doctor and nurses.

If you are a suspect in a child abuse or child molestation case and decide you want to seek the services of a medical doctor or psychiatrist for therapy or treatment, you would think everything you say is confidential. It would seem in the public interest, and certainly in your own best interests, that you be allowed to seek the services of a therapist. Unfortunately, this is not true.

The powerful Division of Family Services helped enact a state law that removes physician-patient privilege in such cases, and the Division of Family Services has the right to examine all your psychiatric or medical reports. Any legally recognized privileged communication, such as physician-patient privilege, does not apply to situations "involving known or suspected child abuse or neglect." This is a terrible law. The loophole is to let your lawyer hire the therapist for you.

Clergy-Penitent Privilege

A confession to your priest or minister is private and confidential.

Informant-Identity Privilege

This privilege is not absolute and may be granted or denied at the discretion of the judge. The name of a snitch might be disclosed if relevant or helpful, although there is no absolute right to disclosure.

The government will claim privilege because it values confidential information given to it. A heavy burden rests on you to prove that the identity of the informant is necessary to your case. You normally lose this argument.

Journalist Privilege

A journalist does have a limited privilege to refuse to testify or answer questions relevant to an investigation into the commission of a crime or to divulge his sources.

The burden is on the moving party to prove:
1. An effort had been made to obtain the information from other sources.
2. The only access to the information is through the journalist.
3. The information is critical to the case.

Most states have a shield law that protects against compelled disclosure of sources and information which allows news announcers and reporters to refuse to testify or answer questions as to the source of their information.

Grand Jury Secrecy

The privileged nature of state and federal grand jury matters prevents grand jurors and lawyers from telling things that occur before a grand jury or revealing that an indictment has been filed.

Accountant-Client Privilege

There is no accountant-client privilege unless the accountant was employed by your attorney and is working under the attorney.

Fifth Amendment Privilege

"Many links frequently compose the chain of testimony which is necessary to convict an individual of a crime ... that no witness be compelled to furnish anyone of them against himself."

—CHIEF JUSTICE JOHN MARSHALL
(1755-1835)
U.S. Supreme Court

A citizen has the unqualified right to take the Fifth Amendment and refuse to answer questions or give information that might form a link in a chain that will tend to incriminate. This includes authenticating records and files if, by identifying or authenticating the records, you tend to incriminate yourself.

There is no Fifth Amendment privilege on behalf of a corporation, especially as to records that are required to be kept by law.

"It's better to keep your mouth shut and appear stupid than to open it and remove all doubt."

—MARK TWAIN

Failure to Talk

"Silence [in court] may be equivalent to confession."

—THE TALMUD, YEVAMOT

If you take the Fifth Amendment as soon as you are arrested, it cannot be used against you at trial. You always have the right to remain silent, and no adverse comment can be made at any time about your decision to exercise your constitutional right.

Rule: When in doubt, take the Fifth Amendment. Your failure to talk cannot be used against you.

Hotline Privilege

Evidence of hotline calls, such as when a person calls the Division of Family Services to report child abuse or neglect, is privileged communication. Over fifty percent of all calls are "unsubstantiated" by the agency's own admission.

Division of Family Services Privileges

This state agency has several statutory privileges that are sufficient to keep taxpayers and interested citizens from finding out where their tax dollars are spent. This is bad law and should be changed. Food stamps, AFDC, welfare, counseling, interviews, and investigations are all hidden by secrecy laws unless your lawyers can file motions for discovery and convince the trial judge to order DFS records opened.

Insured-Insuror Privilege

Anything you say to your insurance adjuster is supposed to be confidential. You are required, under your policy, to cooperate. But if you do, make sure you get a copy of your statement and that your adjuster agrees to confidentiality.

Bail Bonds

"Excessive bail shall not be required, nor excessive fines imposed, nor cruel and unusual punishments inflicted."
—EIGHT AMENDMENT
U.S. Constitution

You have the right to a reasonable bail set by the court, unless the charge is murder. After conviction, bail is often increased since it may be more probable you would fail to appear.

The bondsman is the one person you like to see after being arrested. He is a licensed businessman who pledges his financial assets to the court to ensure that you do not have to remain unjustly imprisoned after arrest and before trial. Courts recognize his importance and dependability by relinquishing you to the bondsman who guarantees your later appearances in court.

The bondsman benefits several people. You are allowed to return to your employment, which is of critical importance when you are the family breadwinner. The family stays together, ensuring the shared support so vital at that time. For a small percentage of the bail amount, the bondsman keeps you from having to pay the full amount of bail. It also helps the sheriff, since it reduces jail population and saves tax-payer costs.

There are five ways to make bail:

1. Hire a bail bondsman (which costs ten percent of the total bond).
2. Pay the full cash amount of bail to the court clerk (the money is later returned).
3. Post a property bond, which normally must meet the following:
   a. The property must be within the county.
   b. An attorney must be hired immediately.
   c. Property abstract, title insurance, and current tax state-ment must be gathered together.
   d. The value of the property should be twice the bond amount.
   e. Proof of value is required from appraisers and real estate experts
   f. Obtain a certified copy of the warranty deed.
4. Post a ten percent cash bond (if the judge consents).
5. Obtain an ROR (release on your own recognizance).

Rule: **If the bond is small, call a bondsman. It's cheap and quick. If the bond is large and you are short of money, wait until your formal arraignment in court. Your lawyer may get the bond lowered or arrange for a property bond or an ROR.**

The U.S. Supreme Court in *Taylor v. Taintor* (1872) said bondsmen can do anything they want, whenever they want, and take you back into custody:

Whenever they choose to do so, may seize you and deliver you up to their discharge; if that cannot be done at once, they may imprison him until it can be done. They may exercise their rights in person or by agent. They may pursue him into another state; they may arrest him on the Sabbath; and, if necessary, may break and enter his house for that purpose. The seizure is not made by virtue of new process. None is needed. It is likened to the rearrest by the sheriff of an escaping prisoner. It is said, "The bail have their principal on a string, and may pull the string whenever they please, and render him in their discharge."

Surrendering on a Warrant

Rule: **Never surrender yourself immediately on your own. If you learn you have an outstanding warrant, contact an attorney for advice.**

Your lawyer should arrange to surrender you into open court session at the earliest opportunity.

If you turn yourself in to the FBI, DEA, highway patrol, or city detectives, you will be questioned and thrown in jail, and a high bond will be recommended. There will be no opportunity to make a property bond, an ROR or have your bond amount lowered. By the time you are taken to court in a smelly, ugly jail uniform, you're upset and fearful.

If you surrender in open court to a judge with your lawyer, your bond might be lowered or more favorable arrangements made. Your lawyer can negotiate a combination of conditions that will reasonably ensure your appearance in court. It will save you money and be more dignified. You can then be routinely booked at a later time, asked routine booking questions, and released.

Should you fail to appear, the court declares the bond in default and issues a *capias warrant* for your arrest. The prosecutor will certify the forfeiture to the Circuit Court for final judgment and execution on the sureties. If the bondsman can later show good reason to have the forfeiture set aside, when you appear he may get his money returned.

Conditions can be placed on you, such as the following:

- Ordering supervision
- Placing restrictions on travel, association, or residence
- Requiring reports to the bailiff at regular intervals
- Requiring a ten percent cash bond
- Forbidding contact with the victim or witnesses
- House arrest or curfew
- Other reasonable conditions

When you're released on bond, your custody is transferred to the bondsman. If you willfully fail to reappear, you are guilty of a separate crime.

Rule: **At a bail hearing, do not concentrate on guilt or innocence or argue. Discuss your previous good record, employment, schooling, family, and strong ties to the community. Affirm that you will responsibly return to court when ordered and obey all court orders.**

Trial Subpoenas

A subpoena is a court-ordered document commanding a person to appear and testify and produce books, papers, or documents. Both federal and state courts allow you to issue subpoenas at a preliminary hearing, at a pretrial suppression hearing, at trial, or at sentencing.

Subpoenas should be issued in good faith and not as a fishing expedition. They should seek documents that are relevant and reasonably procurable in advance of trial. Sometimes the defendant must show that he is unable to properly present his case without production and inspection of the evidence in advance of trial (*U.S. v. Richard Nixon*, 1974).

Especially in state court, the wise defense attorney will make liberal use of subpoenas, bringing in adverse witnesses at a preliminary hearing or pretrial motions to learn the extent of unfavorable and damaging testimony and plan how to counter the evidence at trial. Your lawyer needs to know just how good (or how bad) your case is.

How to Handle Children Who Commit Crimes

Our legal system is trying to find the correct way to try juveniles charged with serious crimes. Time and life itself are alien concepts to thirteen-year-olds who cannot think past the weekend.

Because minors have skewed judgment, we limit their right to vote, drink, drive, join the armed forces, enter into contracts, marry, and other things.

Juvenile court judge, not prosecutors or police, should decide whether children charged with crimes should be tried as adults and not children. Minors should responsible for their acts but we still need to recognize they are children.

In Missouri, a child sixteen years old and under is a minor. He attains the age of responsibility and adulthood, in criminal law terms, at the age of seventeen.

If a child commits crime, a juvenile court judge looks to a number of factors to see wether the child should be "certified" to stand trial as an adult including the seriousness of the crime, the maturity of the child, and whether there are existing beneficial programs that would help the child.

If the child is certified as an adult, he is required to stand trial and go through the adult criminal process as though he were an adult, but he can be sentenced to dual jurisdiction with the State Division of Youth Services. Juvenile facilities are more like high schools and less like prisons and are normally equipped with computers, televisions, sports, and game facilities. There is more freedom and less security than a regular prison.

Once the child reaches seventeen, the Circuit judge has a hearing to determine whether the child should remain in the juvenile facility, be paroled, or serve the remainder of his sentence in a regular prison.

Juveniles

Special courts have exclusive jurisdiction of all crimes where a juvenile (under seventeen) is involved. In misdemeanor violations, the child is released to the parents. In more serious crimes, the child is ordered to a juvenile detention home.

The court holds a hearing within four days. The child may not be held more than seven days unless a formal petition is filed.

Proceedings prior to the juvenile petition are detention hearings. The court receives testimony relevant to the necessity for detention. The court may review written and social reports and appoint a guardian *ad litem*.

Rule: **The juvenile officer may make informal adjustments by giving advice to the juvenile, referring him to appropriate public or private agencies that provide counseling.**

If a formal petition is filed, the juvenile is entitled to be represented by an attorney. A juvenile hearing is not open to the public, and persons are present only if they have a direct interest in the case. The case is decided by the judge—and must be proved beyond a reasonable doubt. The juvenile is afforded rights during the trial and, if convicted, has the right of appeal, similar to regular criminal trials.

Strict adherence to constitutional safeguards, such as *Miranda* warnings, is not required because of the informal nature of juvenile procedures. Juvenile files are secret and can never be opened.

When police determine that an arrested person is a juvenile, he is taken immediately to a juvenile officer and not released until a juvenile judge has ordered the release.

Courtroom Demeanor

**"When I use a word it means just what I choose it to mean—
neither more nor less."**
——HUMPTY DUMPTY
in *Alice Adventures in
Wonderland* by Lewis Carroll

A criminal trial is a serious event. Our system strives to guarantee a fair trial by an impartial judge and jury; and represents the entire history of democratic process and its achievement of individual freedoms. Demeanor in the court must reflect not only a serious attitude but an appreciation of the proceedings, and it demands respect in every word and deed.

Your performance in court will be seriously judged by the jury:

- *Appearance.* Be clean, well groomed, shaved, and conservatively dressed.
- *Demeanor.* A sincere, businesslike attitude should always be displayed, demonstrating a positive, decisive, and knowledgeable attitude. Proper manners are essential.
- *Language.* Slang, profanity, or coarse language should never be used.

The prosecutor will first ask questions on direct examination to relate facts to the court and jury as firsthand knowledge. After the direct, the defense will cross-examine. The functions are as follows:

- To bring out the whole truth and not just facts favorable to the prosecution
- To uncover omissions in testimony that have the effect of leaving unfair or misinterpreted conceptions
- To bring out bias
- To demonstrate uncertainty
- To show unfamiliarity with facts
- To show prejudice

If you are telling the truth, you will be successful under the most rigorous cross-examination. You should not only be sure to tell the truth but also know the limits of your knowledge. Always be alert for leading questions (questions that suggest the expected answer).

Trial Objections

"Good intentions will always be pleaded for every assumption of power . . . (The) Constitution was made to guard the people against the dangers of good intentions. There are men in all ages who mean to govern well, but they mean to govern. They promise to be good masters, but they mean to be masters."

—DANIEL WEBSTER (1782-1852)

During the jury trial, both lawyers will voice various objections. If an objection is *sustained*, then the question is to be disregarded and the answer shall not be considered in evidence. If the objection is *overruled*, the judge does not find merit in the objection and the answer is for the jury to consider. Some common objections are as follows:

- *Argumentative.* When an attorney argues with the witness.
- *Asked and answered.* A later repetition of the same question calling for the same answer.
- *Assuming facts not in evidence.* The framing of a question in such a manner that certain facts not in evidence must be assumed as true by the witness before answering.
- *Bolstering.* A question that attempts to bolster testimony before the testimony is attacked, such as, "You are telling me the truth, aren't you?"
- *Best evidence rule.* The best documentary evidence available and procurable must be admitted, as opposed to secondary documentary evidence, such as, "What does the contract say?"
- *Beyond the scope.* Testimony outside the scope of inquiry. Often the objection is raised on cross-examination and pertains to facts not brought out on direct examination.
- *Calling for conclusion.* Questioning where a conclusion" must be drawn from the question before it can be answered. "Isn't it a fact?" or "As a matter of fact," and similar questions call for a conclusion.
- *Compound question.* A question requiring a number of answers.
- *Cumulative.* Seeking repetitious evidence that is unnecessary.
- *Hearsay.* Testimony that rests on the truthfulness of someone not on the witness stand, or of the second source, rather than firsthand evidence. Hearsay is secondary indirect evidence and is based on what a third party has told the witness.

EXAMPLE: **Witness A testifies to the truth of Fact X because B told A it was true. This testimony is inadmissible because B is not available to testify and be cross-examined, observed, or judged by the court, and is not under oath.**

The hearsay rule has many exceptions which may allow the evidence under some other theory. The rationale underlying exceptions embraces (1) the necessity for the exception to serve the ends of justice; and (2) the guarantee of trustworthiness of evidence.

Out-of-court statements made by persons who were not involved in a trial may not be admitted into evidence for the truth of what was said. However, such information may come into evidence for the purpose of explaining conduct and other exceptions.

Other hearsay exceptions include the following:

- Excited utterance
- Then-existing feelings
- For diagnosis or treatment
- Recorded recollections
- Regular records
- Absence of expected regular record entry
- Public records
- Absence of a public record
- Vital statistics
- Church records
- Marriage, birth, and death certificates
- Family records
- Property records
- Ancient documents
- Market publications
- Learned treatises
- Pedigree reputation
- History and boundary reputation
- Character reputation
- Conviction of a crime
- Judgment
- Dying declarations
- Statement against interest
- *Leading questions* suggest the answer. They are permitted only:
  1. On cross-examination
  2. When a witness is hostile or adverse
  3. When the witness is a: child
  4. If the witness' memory needs to be refreshed

- *Improper foundation.* A proper foundation must be laid before facts are admitted into evidence. In the instance of photographs, the laying of proper foundation includes the date and time photographs were taken and whether the picture accurately represents the scene as it was when the picture was taken.
- *Improper impeachment of own witness.* You cannot argue with your own witness unless he gives surprise or hostile testimony.
- *Invades the provision of the jury.* Calling for an answer on the ultimate issue or fact that the jury is to determine.
- *No corpus delicti.* Offering facts into evidence before proof that a crime has been committed.
- *Prejudicial.* Evidence that unnecessarily inflames the passions of the jury, such as bloody photographs or evidence of another unrelated crime.
- *Self-serving.* Evidence may not be offered that only furthers the witness's own cause.
- *Strike.* Delete and remove from the official court record.

Rule: I've rarely found it beneficial to repeatedly jump up and down and make technical objections in front of a jury. Juries grow weary of lawyers constantly interrupting witnesses. Jurors give their precious time as a part of their duty and they wish to simply hear the evidence and make an informed decision. Hearing lawyers wrangle over fine points of law is a travesty on the system of justice. Little is gained by a constant barrage of objections. Occasionally, an objection will tend to show that the judge is on my side (if I win my objection), disrupt opposing counsel's train of thought and rattle him in front of the jury, or show that the opposing counsel is not well prepared. *The fewer objections, the better.*

The Ten Commandments of Cross-Examination

"He can run, but he can't hide."
—JOE LOUIS (1914-1981)

"Never, never, never, on cross-examination, ask a witness a question you don't already know the answer to, was a tenet I absorbed with my baby food. Do it, and you'll often get an answer you don't want."
—ATTICUS FINCH, in Harper Lee's *To Kill a Mockingbird*

Once a witness testifies, he is subject to full cross-examination by the opposing lawyer. Attorneys have the right of cross-examination of witnesses within proper bounds. The scope of cross-examination is limited to matters brought out in the direct examination, and only in rare cases may new evidence be introduced.

An attack on the believability of a witness is called *impeachment*. Discrediting a witness may be accomplished as follows:

- Showing bias or prejudice
- Showing incapacity as a witness
- Showing bad reputation for honesty
- Showing conviction of a crime
- Proof of prior inconsistent statements
- Showing facts inconsistent with his testimony
- Showing he has been promised money, leniency, or favors
- Showing motive or reason to lie or favor

There are important rules lawyers use in cross-examination:

- Be brief.
- Ask short questions using plain words.
- Ask only leading questions.
- Don't ask a question if you don't know the answer.
- Listen to the answer.
- Don't quarrel with the witness.
- Don't permit the witness to explain.
- Don't allow the witness to repeat direct testimony.
- Avoid asking the "one question too many."
- Save the explanation for summation.

A lawyer should not be afraid to cross-examine, to fail, or to be embarrassed. It will occur no matter how experienced an attorney is.

You never know what is going to happen when a witness takes the stand, and it is an extremely rare fight when both sides don't land at least a few punches.

A lawyer will try to control by controlling the questions. If he succeeds, he can control the outcome of the case.

Rule: **Never ask a question if you don't already know the answer.**

Stare Decisis

"It is revolting to have no better reason for a rule of law than that so it was laid down in the time of Henry IV."
—OLIVER WENDELL HOLMES
(1841-1935) Chief Justice,
U.S. Supreme Court

The cornerstone of our legal system is that prior judgments and court opinions, sound in principle and workable in practice, are heavily relied upon in the law and are cited by lawyers and judges as legal authority. In deciding legal questions, courts look for prior case decisions to see whether a nearly identical case has been decided answering the same legal question (the doctrine of *stare decisis*).

This does not mean that courts refrain from reconsideration of prior decisions. Legal research by lawyers and judges can take many hours or days to determine minute points of law, checking prior court decisions in other states and all federal courts throughout the United States.

Lawyers look for cases to prove precedent. If they can find an identical case, they have a much better chance of persuading the judge. A *white horse case* is one that is identical; a *case on all fours* is exactly opposite. Supporting or distinguishing authority is cited in legal briefs and supplied to the opposing lawyer.

The Closing Argument

"It's never over till it's over."
—YOGI BERRA (1925-)
New York Yankees, 1946

"Good idea not to accept gold medal until race is won."
—CHARLIE CHAN

"Among attorneys in Tennessee the saying is: 'When you have the facts on your side, argue the facts. When you have the law on your side, argue the law. When you have neither, holler.'"
—ALBERT GORE, JR. (1948-)

Closing arguments are the time for the trial attorney to show his colors. Nothing could be more boring than an attorney who reads his closing statement from typewritten pages or who merely reviews the testimony of the witnesses. The lawyer must argue from the facts.

An attorney should proceed to the lectern and argue with a minimum of prepared notes. Juries are impressed by the attorney who speaks from the heart, who knows enough about his case that he can call the witnesses' names and argue their testimony without the use of notes.

Even the most complicated case can be reduced to attacks on the credibility of key witnesses, demonstration of false reliance by the prosecutor on the evidence, or proof by the defendant's witnesses that may be enough to raise a reasonable doubt.

Sentencing Hearing

State Court jury trials require a separate *bifucated trial* for sentencing.

There is the *first stage* of the trial to determine guilt or innocence. If found guilty, then a separate second trial is held—complete with opening and closing statements (and presentation of evidence) to determine punishment.

If you have a prior felony record which has resulted in actual imprisonment for more than 120 days, then the judge will do the sentencing and not the jury.

At the *second stage,* evidence supporting or mitigating punishment will be offered including (1) the impact of the crime upon the victim, the victim's family and others; (2) the nature and circumstances of the offenses; and (3) the history and character of the defendant.

You may waive your right for jury sentencing and let the judge sentence you if you wish.

If you are proved to be a prior, persistent or dangerous offender, then the sentencing must be by the judge. If you have one previous prison commitment, you must serve 40 percent of your sentence. If there are two or more previous commitments, you must serve 50 percent and if three or more, you must serve 80 percent.

If you are convicted of one of the nine (9) deadly sins laws (crimes designated by the legislature to be serious offenses), then you must serve 85 percent of your time. Life imprisonment is defined as 30 years.

Allocution

"Through patience a ruler can be persuaded,
and a gentle tongue can break a bone."
—Proverbs 25: 15

You stand before a grim, godlike judge. You have been dreading this moment for months, if not years. The lawyer has prepared you for sentencing as best he could, but the awful reality has now set in and you are shaking.

The judge, in a monotone, goes through the script: "Have you read the Presentence Report? Do you have any questions? Before sentence is pronounced, do you have any statements that you would like to make?"

It is a time-honored and symbolic rite now enshrined in both state and federal law. It is the sole opportunity for you to have the last word, the final chance to say something, anything, to influence the judge, to present a human face before final sentencing. It is a chance to gain self-respect before sentence is imposed.

Recent surveys of judges indicate that allocution can, in fact, make a difference. It might save a few years or perhaps just a few months. You should consider the following: do no harm; have a theme; be brief; be prepared; and express remorse.

Remember first to accept responsibility. Do yourself no harm. For every argument you make, the prosecutor has an answer.

Your allocution should have a theme. If it is a drug case, perhaps it is your addiction to drugs that led you to this state of affairs. Perhaps it is family, or friends, or society.

We live in a world of shortened attention spans. There is a heavy court docket, and sentences are scheduled through a calendar. A judge will not take kindly to a speech that goes for a lengthy period of time. Shorter is better.

Be prepared. Word-for-word scripting is unnecessary because it looks stilted. Rehearse prior to the day of sentencing and speak from the heart. You should start by setting the tone by expressing remorse. Discuss your understanding of, and willingness to abide by, court alternatives to imprisonment, including home detention, placement in a halfway house, supervised release, enrollment in a drug treatment or drug education program, community service, or paying a fine.

The judge expects to hear remorse and regret. Don't whine, blame others, or harangue against law enforcement, confidential informants, or crime victims. It will be counterproductive. Your apology must be unconditional.

If the victim is in the courtroom, turn and apologize to the victim and his family. They are expressing rage and anger at the crime and asking for the harshest possible punishment. Victims always state that the defendant never apologized. Take the wind out of their sails. Turn around and apologize.

Allocution cannot be left to the last moment for sudden inspiration or improvisation. It should be worked at, practiced, and treated with respect. Even if it falls on deaf ears, you will at least have a chance to express your self-respect and to stand as an individual before the court. If nothing else, you clothe yourself with dignity.

Dismissal of Charges

If you are charged but the case is later dismissed (*nolle proseque*) or you are found not guilty or given a suspended sentence, all court records are closed.

You cannot thereafter be guilty of perjury for giving a false statement by reason of failure to recite the arrest or trial in response to any inquiry made for any purpose (such as employment applications).

Mistrials

Once a trial has started and the jury selected is sworn, it is possible for the trial judge to grant a mistrial where there is a manifest necessity. The trial is immediately terminated (prior to verdict) and the case rescheduled for jury trial at a future date. There is no double jeopardy protection unless prosecutorial misconduct provoked the mistrial.

A typical example of a mistrial is a hung jury where a jury is hopelessly deadlocked and cannot reach a verdict or when illegal or prejudiced evidence is accidentally placed before the jury.

If in the process of the trial you believe you are winning the case, then you do not want a mistrial granted. If the case is rescheduled, the prosecutor may bring forth additional witnesses or do a better job the second time. I you believe you are losing the case, a motion for mistrial is a wise move since the case will be rescheduled for trial in the future and the state's case may grow weaker.

Right of Appeal

If the jury returns a verdict of guilty, the judge will give you approximately thirty days to file a Motion for New Trial and to possibly order the Missouri Board of Probation and Parole to complete a Sentencing Assessment Report. You will argue that a new trial should be granted due to trial errors and mistakes.

Most post-trial arguments are overruled, allocution granted, and sentencing pronounced. You have the right of appeal to the next higher court (the Missouri Court of Appeals).

If you chose to appeal, a transcript is prepared by the court reporter, a legal file is assembled of all the court pleadings and docket sheets, and your attorney researches the law and files a lengthy legal brief. The brief will be orally argued before the Court of Appeals or Missouri Supreme Court.

Although you have the right of appeal, most appeals are subsequently rejected and the guilty sentence affirmed.

A common misbelief is that additional new evidence can be presented or argued. In fact, you are bound by your allegations in the Motion for New Trial and nothing additional can be argued.

You have the right to file an appeal within ten days of formal sentencing because of allegations of reversible error. This means a mistake was committed by the judge and the error was so harmful that you did not get a fair trial and are therefore entitled to a new trial.

If found guilty; you might claim that:

1. There is not sufficient evidence to find you guilty and the verdict should be reversed.
2. Prejudicial evidence was used.
3. The judge made irreversible errors in his rulings on objections and pretrial motions.
4. The prosecutor knowingly used perjured evidence or refused to disclose favorable evidence.
5. Your lawyer was incompetent, based on community standards.
6. Numerous Sixth Amendment violations occurred that denied you a fair trial.

Many prosecutors deliberately create error for the purpose of getting convictions, relying on the hope that appellate courts will find their error harmless and that the conviction will stand (and most do). The doctrine of harmless error has seriously undermined our legal system.

Privacy of Arrest Records

Arrest records are supposed to be private if you are not charged within a few days after arrest—unless you give consent for someone to look at your records.

Police always have access to the records. It is possible to ask the court to expunge the arrest records, since courts have considerable equitable powers, but unless good reasons exist, courts are reluctant to erase them. They remain law enforcement records forever.

Rule: **Forget about having your arrest records expunged at the police station. It isn't going to happen.**

Free Speech

"Free speech means the right to yell 'theater' in a crowded fire."
—ABBIE HOFFMAN (1936-1989)

"Between two evils, I always pick the one I've never tried before."
—MAE WEST (1892-1980)

You can't yell "fire" when nothing is burning but does the First Amendment give citizens a blank check? There are certain exceptions to free speech:

Libel and Slander

You may be sued for damages if you spread a defamatory falsehood in print (libel) or with spoken words and gestures (slander).

The burden of proof varies, depending upon whether the person suing you is a private citizen or a public figure (a government official, celebrity, or community leader). Public figures must prove that the defamation not only was false but was made with actual malice or reckless disregard for the truth. Statements of opinion are usually deemed fair comment; the Supreme Court has held that there is no such thing as a false idea.

Obscenity

For decades, courts have wrestled with laws defining obscenity and pornography attempting to draw the fine line to protect First Amendment rights but to isolate hardcore pornography.

The amendment guarantees the right of free speech, which, through the Fourteenth Amendment, protects citizens of each state.

Search warrants authorizing mass seizures of books and magazines raise a special problem: they must not operate as a prior restraint on protected reading materials. A prior adversary hearing before the seizure, or a prompt postdelivery hearing, is required.

What is obscene depends on the following factors:

1. Whether the average person, applying contemporary community standards, finds that the work, taken as a whole, appeals to prurient interests
2. Whether it describes in a patently offensive way sexual conduct specifically defined by state law
3. Whether it lacks serious literary, artistic, political, or scientific value.
4. The jury is entitled to rely on its knowledge of contemporary community standards.

Rule: **Nudity itself, the naked male or female body, is not obscene.**

Immunity

The prosecuting attorney has the legal power to give a person immunity from prosecution for past crimes in return for his testimony and cooperation in ongoing criminal investigations targeting others. Transactional immunity is normally conditioned upon full and truthful future testimony and presents a shield against virtually any possibility of future prosecution.

Immunity assures you only that your testimony will not be used against you later, leaving prosecutors free to move against you with evidence supposedly obtained independently. Needless to say, if you give them evidence the police does not know about, it can then be used against you. Therefore the use of immunity is of little value.

Testimony of Children

Children are allowed to testify if it is shown that they are capable of receiving just impressions of the facts and relating them and they understand the importance of telling the truth.

Children under twelve can testify in sexual abuse cases by video recording statement either if they are unavailable or if there would be significant emotional or psychological trauma if the child testified.

A child can actually testify at a jury trial from hearsay testimony of others, or by videotape about statements given to school teachers, police officers, juvenile workers, nurses, doctors, and social workers. The defendant still has the right to subpoena the child for crossexamination purposes. It is extremely difficult to defend a child abuse charge because hearsay statements of the child will come into evidence (known as a 491 Hearing).

> "If you can't stand the heat, stay out of the kitchen."
> —HARRY S. TRUMAN (1884-1972)

> "If you know your enemy and know yourself, you need not fear the result of a hundred battles."
> —SUN TZU (544-496 B.C.)

Victim's Rights

Missouri passed a Victim's Rights Law automatically affording strong constitutional rights to victims and their families. This includes the right to be informed about the status off any case, the right to information about the alleged crime, to be informed in a timely manner of all court dates and to be present at bail reduction hearings unless in the determination of the court the interest of justice require otherwise. *RSMO 595.209.1 (4)*

The Missouri Legislature, in it's zeal to be politically correct and popular with Victim's Rights lobby groups have even gone so far as to legislate the rights of the victims "are absolute and the policy of this

State is that the victim's rights are *paramount to the defendant's rights*," (which is impossible). *RSMO 595.209.5 (2007)*

If a person is found to have a "mental abnormality or personality disorder" may be viewed as a dangerous sexual offender if it's difficult or impossible for the person to control his behavior.

In such cases involuntary civil commitment may occur (*Kansas vs. Crane, 2002*).

The Adam Walsh Act is one of the most complex, progressive and punitive sex offender laws ever enacted responding to a public and political outcry of concern over sex offenders.

The civil commitment objectives also have a profound impact effect on many Federal sex offenders. If a person is deemed to be a "sexually dangerous person" then a battle of the experts pursues and a person can be confined long after the end of the prison sentence.

Tricks Prosecutors Play

"If there were no bad people there would be no good lawyers."
—CHARLES DICKENS

"The natural progress of things is for liberty to yield and government to gain ground."
—THOMAS JEFFERSON (1743-1820)

The prosecutor may be earnest and prosecute with great vigor— indeed he should do so. But while he may strike hard blows, he is not at liberty to strike foul ones. It is as much his duty to refrain from improper methods calculated to produce wrongful convictions as it is to use every legitimate means to bring about a just one.

Most prosecutors are extremely honest, ethical, and hard working. They get an occasional edge over the defense lawyer, but this is OK. All's fair in war. If you are charged with a crime, you will be fortunate to have a fair and honest prosecutor opposing you and not one who hides evidence.

Some prosecutors, however, go too far. They take it personally. They hide evidence, withhold information, bluff, leak to the press, and tell you less than the whole truth.

Prosecutors wield great power and sometimes engage in misconduct. They are less subject than defense attorneys to judicial or bar association oversight. Some types of prosecutorial misconduct hav become commonplace.

Undeterred prosecutorial discretion is terrifying:

1. Prosecutors are perceived by juries as prestigious and honorable.
2. They have powerful strategic and financial resources that give them distinct advantages.
3. They enjoy great decision-making powers (charging crimes, plea bargaining, granting immunity, subpoenaing witnesses to grand juries, and determining sentences).
4. Prosecutors are elected to political office by the very persons sitting on the jury.

Role of the Prosecuting Attorney

"I put my trust in God, not U.S. Attorneys."
—BILL GINSBERG (1999)
Attorney

"A government is the only known vessel that leaks from the top."
—JAMES RESTON (1909-1995)
Political commentator

The prosecuting attorney is obliged to choose his case; he should not choose his *target*. The most dangerous power of the prosecutor is that he will pick people he thinks he should get rather than cases that need to be prosecuted. A prosecutor stands a fair chance of finding at least a technical violation of some act on the part of almost anyone. Thus, it may not be a question of discovering the commission of a crime and then looking for the man who committed it, it is a question of picking the man and then searching the law books or putting investigators to work to pin some offense on him. The prosecutor can pick a person whom he dislikes or desires to embarrass, or select some group of unpopular persons, and then look for an offense. The greatest danger of abuse of prosecuting power lies in the fact that some prosecutors get downright personal.

Instead of clamping down on prosecutorial misconduct and imposing remedies of reversal of convictions or dismissal of charges, appellate courts use the harmless error review (concluding that although the prosecutor erred, it did not affect the jury verdict), overlooking misconduct (claiming that it was invited by the defense lawyer), ignoring misconduct where the defense lawyer failed to formally object, or indulging in the fiction of curative instructions (the judge tells the jury to disregard and not consider what they have just heard—similar to telling you about elephants, and then telling you not to think about elephants).

Tricks that prosecutors use include the following:

- *Manipulation of the media.* The prosecutor and media have a cozy relationship: the prosecutor releases prejudicial information to them, and they print it, attributing it to "unnamed sources." The result is a slanted story trying the accused in the court of public opinion. Quoting the results of scientific tests and statements of witnesses helps form the public's decision about guilt before any of the evidence is ever introduced into court. Some evidence cited in newspapers may not even be legally admissible. The news media and the prosecutor need each other. Media need to fill news space every day, and sometimes beg for interesting news stories. The prosecutor may want his name in headlines. It will help his reputation and his next political race.

- *Assassinating your character.* Attacking your character makes a conviction more likely. The prosecutor may portray you as dangerous or undesirable or allege that you associate with bad persons, inferring that you have a criminal record and are likely to have committed the crime.
- *Introducing improper evidence.* False, misleading, or inadmissible evidence deceives the jury.
- *Inflaming juror prejudice.* Prosecutors sometimes appeal to passions and prejudices by placing inadmissible evidence before juries, offering gruesome photographs or using inflammatory rhetoric, exhorting juries to "win the war on crime," inciting them to vengeance, or indirectly appealing to racial, ethnic, national, or religious prejudice or to wealth or class bias.
- *Violating the privilege against self-incrimination.* It is improper to infer because of your silence at trial, or failure to explain conduct to police after arrest, that you should be assumed guilty. Prosecutors come as close as they can, stating their own case as uncontradicted or unrequited (an indirect reference to your failure to testify).
- *Name-calling* against your lawyer. Everybody dislikes criminal defense lawyers, so attacking your lawyer can be effective. Attacks on the defense lawyer are quite usual—belittling him, gaining an advantage before the jury by running him down, claiming that his objections were made in bad faith or that he always uses the same defense, does not care about the case, or has no confidence in his own client. Kill the messenger!
- *Sandbagging.* The prosecutor makes new arguments and raises new theories for the first time during rebuttal summation so your lawyer has no chance to answer.
- *Exploiting prosecutorial prestige.* Prosecutors may stress their own personal integrity and that of their office by arguing that they represent "the people" and are merely prosecuting a charge "brought by a grand jury." They insinuate that their case is truthful and improperly vouch for their witnesses.
- *Misrepresenting the record.* Prosecutors often refer to matters outside the record, not entered into evidence, implying that

they are incriminating issues of fact. They refer to the avail-ability of pardon, executive clemency, or appellate review. They encourage the jury to go ahead and convict, suggesting that if there is any error, a later appellate court can correct it. This lessens the jurors' sense of responsibility.

- *Hiding evidence.* Rules require all police reports to be turned over immediately to defense counsel, but often they are hidden. The defense lawyer will learn of information that might be helpful, but not until it is too late. On appeal, the burden is on your lawyer to show that the evidence was likely to make a difference in the jury verdict.

- Once you win a case, the prosecutor has unbridled discretion *in filing new charges,* and can keep refiling almost without limit. He can plea bargain and make unbelievable sweetheart deals with other criminals to force them to testify against you with-out restriction.

- *Talking to Probation and Parole.* If you plead guilty, a Presen-tence Report is filed with the court. The prosecutor will give his version of your case to the PSI writer, whether he can prove it or not. Watch out! They have a cozy relationship.

- *Talking during a bond study.* Sometimes the judge orders a bond study to help make a decision about the amount of your bond. The probation officer doing the study may talk to the prosecu-tor. Look out!

- *Upsetting your family.* The prosecutor can subpoena friends, family, and business customers and imply all manner of things to them. An unscrupulous prosecutor will ruin your life unless you are strong willed.

The Cozy Duo

"If it bleeds, it leads."
—NEWS MEDIA AXIOM

The prosecutor can screw you royally in the media. He has access to reporters and they curry each other's favor. Reporters need the prosecutors to leak their stories. It helps their job.

The prosecutor needs the media because he wants to be viewed as tough on crime. He is running for re-election or for judge. He gets free advertising and is viewed as being tough.

Reporters will quote informed sources. Who in the world are these sources? They will quote police reports. How do reporters get police reports, especially before the defense lawyer does?

The prosecutor, by law, is only supposed to release certain limited things, things that do not prejudice you. Do not count on it. Once your case is completed and you plead guilty and have been sentenced, the prosecutor will fax press releases out so fast it will make your head swim.

Unless your lawyer is on his toes and calls the prosecutor's hand, you and your family may suffer from a great deal of bad publicity.

Curbing Prosecutorial Excess

The phrase *prosecutorial discretion* once conjured up an image of sober, reflective, and mature exercise of well-informed judgment. There was public confidence in the system.

Now the phrase has become virtually synonymous with arbitrary targeting of suspects based on criteria ranging from political hardball to prosecutorial ambition to the allure of newspaper headlines and television promos that can grace a faceless civil servant with instant celebrity status, much like magic pixie dust. Large prosecutors' offices retain press agents and spin doctors.

Destruction of Evidence

Under the Due Process Clause of the Fourteenth Amendment, criminal prosecutions are guided by fundamental fairness. You have a meaningful opportunity to present a complete defense (constitutionally guaranteed access to evidence) that protects you from an erroneous conviction and ensures the integrity of the justice system.

If the prosecutor loses evidence, destroys evidence prior to trial that may be material to guilt or punishment, or hides evidence, then your case should be dismissed (*Brady v. Maryland*, 1963), especially if the prosecutor acts in bad faith.

Arizona v. Youngblood (1988) directs the judge to weigh several factors:

1. Whether the evidence was lost while in the government's custody
2. Whether the government acted in disregard for the accused
3. Whether the government was negligent in failing to have established standards of care
4. Whether the acts were deliberate or accidental
5. To what extent police officers were involved
6. Whether the prosecutor participated in the destruction

The evidence is considered material only if there was a reasonable probability that its disclosure would have altered the result of the proceeding.

Before You Agree to Cooperate

"If you can dream it, you can do it."
—WALT DISNEY (1901-1966)

If you possess information to help the government investigate or prosecute another person, you should be highly motivated to enter into a cooperation agreement with the U.S. Attorney. The prosecutor can recommend a downward departure under sentencing Rule SK1.1 on the basis that you provided substantial assistance.

Once you make known the fact you are willing to cooperate, an informal meeting is held with the prosecutor or U.S. Attorney and the investigating agent to see whether you might be helpful. A proffer agreement is signed wherein the prosecutor agrees that all information given shall remain confidential and not be used against you at trial.

If the information is helpful, the sentencing judge has the authority to impose a sentence below a level established by statute or the Federal Sentencing Guidelines. This is the only mechanism to allow sentences below the statutory mandatory minimum of the Guidelines. Also, the judge can sentence you to less time than a statutory minimum under the *safety valve* law.

The proffer agreement affords you limited protection. It keeps the information from being used against you at sentencing or in formulating new charges. The government can still build an independent case based on proffered information.

None of your statements can be used at trial, but the government may still cross-examine you should your trial testimony contradict statements made during a proffer.

A Snitch in Time

Rule: **Nobody talks, everybody walks.**

In federal court, it is especially important to accept responsibility for criminal conduct. If you assist or cooperate with prosecutors in some way, it will reduce your sentence on the complicated Sentencing Guideline scale, which means less time in prison.

Some people make a career out of snitching. They routinely break the law and when pinched, they roll over and cooperate with the police. Government handlers recruit criminals for the snitch business and try to put a favorable spin on their credibility. They become star witnesses and testify against former friends; then they plead guilty to lesser charges so they don't have to spend the rest of their lives in jail.

By breaking the code of silence, the feds push a noble view of their man, and the snitch brokers himself a chance at a rebirth as a law-abiding citizen. Being a snitch is dirty business. Tattling on your best friends, talking behind their backs, and causing them to be arrested and charged with a crime will not leave a good taste in your mouth.

If you are sentenced to imprisonment, up to one year later you can request your sentence be reduced (Rule 35) for your successful snitching.

Accomplice Testimony

Accomplices may testify against each other as long as they are not co-defendants in the same criminal case. Where an accomplice has given a confession and testifies, the confession is admissible against him. However, that portion of his confession implicating another de-

107

fendant must be cut out or erased under the *Bruton rule*.

Rule: **You can be convicted on your confession, but not by the confession of another person on trial with you.**

Snitching 101

"A government witness who has been demanding twenty-four hour protection today was given a roll-on deodorant."
— GEORGE CARLIN
Napalm and Silly Putty (2001)

"I hate to say this, Sammy, but maybe you should cooperate."
— EDDIE GARAFOLA TO SAMMY "THE BULL" GRAVANO before testifying against John Gotti (1991)

You've been arrested, your house is searched, and the pressure is on. You are soon to be charged with a crime—your good name ruined by the media. You are facing massive attorney fees, loss of your job, and disrespect and ridicule from everywhere. The cops tell you, "There is a way out." What are the rules for cooperating?

- *Get advice.* Consult a knowledgeable lawyer, one who has been down the road with other informants. Make sure he can cooperate with police and doesn't object to representing you. Listen to his advice as he weighs the pros and cons about your life as a snitch. See what he recommends. There are several ways to skin a cat!
- *Tell the truth.* If you do cooperate and meet with the police, tell the truth. Don't start out by lying and trying to mislead the cops about your involvement and that of your friends. They know better. They will discover your lies. Federal law prohibits making a false statement *(18 USC, Sec 1001).*
- *Hit and run.* See if you can give them just enough accurate information, enough to make them happy, so they will leave you

alone. If their case against you is average, the cops may be happy with a few tidbits of leftover information and let you go.

- *Act secretly.* See if you can act as a confidential informant (CI) without your name being broadcast to the world. Give confidential but reliable information. Police will check it out to confirm your truthfulness. Then they obtain search warrants using you only as a reliable confidential informant. Maybe no one will ever know your identity.

- *Introduce.* The next best thing is to introduce. The cops will assign an unassuming narc to you who fits right in and will be your companion, Joe, from out of town. Your job is to introduce him around as a trusted high roller who has connections.

- *Let your fingers do the walking.* Try to make telephone calls. The cops will wire your phone while you call friends and engage them in incriminating conversations. They love to make tape recordings.

- *Wearing a wire.* The most dangerous thing you can do is to wear a wire. It could be an invitation to the morgue. If you are deeply involved enough that the only way out is to be the front man, wear a Sony, Nagra, or other high-quality tape recorder that records and transmits to waiting cops. They monitor and move in when the deal goes down. Imagine being searched by a drug seller when he finds you are a police informant. Good luck and have fun!

- *How long is this hell?* Repeated buys. How long must you work? Cops will want you to make buy after buy. They will bleed you dry if you let them. They let you work for months, making dozens of cases, dangling carrots in your grasp, suggesting they will "inform the prosecutor of your cooperation" (that, plus fifty cents, will get you a cup of *coffee*), and other good things. Ask for their promises in writing and watch them run in the opposite direction. (Cops will never put anything in writing since they do not make the decisions—the prosecutor and judge are the bosses.)

Cops want you to turn several tricks with an equal or higher quantity of drugs than the amount for which you were originally arrested.

Don't try to make deals with them without your attorney. If they tell you not to get an attorney, you can get them fired.

Rule No.1: **Talk to your lawyer** *before* **you meet with police. Don't let police scare you out of getting advice.**

Rule No.2: **Strike the best deal you can, minimizing your involvement. Let your lawyer deal with the prosecutor who has the authority to make deals.**

Rule No.3: **Try to satisfy the cops with confidential "background information" so your name is not made public.**

Rule No.4: **Get in and get out quickly. Ideally, within several weeks, after one or two deals, you are out with a free ride and get what you want.**

Rule No.5: **The cops will use good guy/bad guy routines. They have no authority to make plea bargains and will speak only in vague, general terms. They will never appear in court with you. They will put nothing in writing.**

Timing Is Everything

The government is always more receptive to individuals who are willing to provide information *early* in the investigation. Valuable time can be lost while you decide what to do. The timeliness of cooperation is one important criterion the judge will consider when deciding whether to give a downward departure. There are many advantages of early cooperation.

Some folks are absolutely opposed to cooperating. Perhaps it is machismo, fear of retribution, or simply wanting no part of testifying against others. I'll remind you of your courage when the prison doors clang shut. Those whom you are protecting would roll on you in a New York minute if they had the chance. Everyone wants to duck and cover to save his own skin.

The Truth, the Whole Truth . . .

Understand the rules of engagement prior to deciding whether to snitch. Cooperation must be complete. You often have to betray friends and family and be prepared to testify against them before the grand jury, at trial, or sentencing.

At a proffer, the government does not want half-truths, omissions, or lies. You may be asked to take a lie detector test. The government has a wealth of information concerning your associates, family, and everyday life, as you may have been under investigation for months or years. If you lie, you can be prosecuted for making a false statement to a federal officer, and your sentence could be increased to include obstruction of justice.

There are no promises of a specific sentence. It is up to the judge. Judges will depart downward to varying degrees on the basis of the value of your cooperation, culpability, prior record, and the crime in question.

Capias Warrants

In the process of various court proceedings, there are a required number of court appearances. Your presence is not required at some court appearances. Nothing of substance is accomplished at some court appearances. Notwithstanding this, if you do not appear and/or your lawyer does not appear, sometimes the judge will go ahead and issue a warrant for your arrest, known as a bench or capias warrant. Some prosecution-oriented judges issue warrants on their own, even when the prosecutor is not present.

This is an annoyance and a harassment. If you are rearrested, you have to spend time in jail and/or waste money with a second bail bondsman. It serves no purpose but harassment. Watch out!

The Multiple Arrest Game

If you are unlucky enough to have drawn the prosecutor's attention, he can have you arrested at least three different times on the exact same charge. You can be arrested late on a Friday night and held over the weekend three times in a row, which will cause you to spend many days in jail, cost you hundreds or thousands of dollars in attorney's fees and bonds, and jeopardize your job:

1. You are arrested on *probable cause*. You can be held up to twenty hours and questioned. If no formal charges are filed, you are released, unless of course, you are lucky enough to post an expensive bond within this time frame.
2. The prosecutor decides to file charges at his whim. When this happens, a criminal complaint is filed with the Associate Circuit Clerk's Office and a warrant is issued. You will be arrested a *second* time, taken to jail, and required to post a bond.
3. Without notice to you, the prosecutor can take a witness secretly before a grand jury (who will testify from hearsay). You will be indicted and charges will be filed against you a *third* time—all for the same offense.

Late Notice of Witnesses

Prosecutors are supposed to give advance notice of the names and addresses of all witnesses they reasonably expect to use at trial. They seldom do and often wait until a few days prior to trial or on the day of trial itself, claiming an oversight. Worse yet, instead of disclosing the witness's address, a prosecutor may tell your attorney to write to the witness in care of the prosecutor's office. This effectively prevents you from learning the address prior to the day of trial (unless you take expensive depositions). Prosecutors hide their witnesses and tell them not to talk with your attorney. It is as though they own the witnesses. Judges traditionally side with the prosecutor and allow late endorsement of witnesses, then give the defense counsel an opportunity to interview the witnesses in the courthouse hallway.

This is the last thing in the world a lawyer is able to do during the pressure and time constraints of a trial. It is impossible to investigate your opponent's case in the hallway while your mind and attention are on other things. Nonetheless, it is a law that is often abused by prosecutors.

Hiding Reports

You will file a written Request for Discovery. The law requires prosecutors disclose all evidence favorable to you.

Prosecutors seldom make a written response to your discovery requests because they do not want to be pinned down. They will normally tell the judge, "We've made our file available." The fact is that many items are not in their files because of design or neglect. This is an abuse of the so-called open file policy.

It is not really open because there are all kinds of reports, bench notes, handwritten notes, test results, memorandums, and faxes. These reside within the witnesses' notes, which the prosecutors do not take the time to obtain.

What is in the prosecutor's file (or what is not) and what the prosecutor claims that your defense counsel has viewed is just another swearing contest. Guess who wins?

At trial, when new evidence is sprung on your lawyer, he will rightly claim surprise! He has never seen the evidence before and it has never been disclosed to him. The prosecutor will exclaim in amazement, "He has had full access to our files." The fact is that evidence and reports often remain with the police, sheriff, highway patrol, or lab technicians. The prosecutor makes no effort until the day of trial to obtain these reports and disclose them to your lawyer.

This is particularly true of expert witnesses who work for the highway patrol or regional crime lab. They never send their field or bench notes to the prosecutor. To adequately cross-examine experts, such notes are needed and are rarely supplied until it is too late. You can't fight what you can't see. It ends up being trial by ambush.

The Sixth Amendment confers upon every accused the right "to be confronted with the witnesses against him," and "to have compulsory process for obtaining witnesses in his favor." The Fifth Amendment also guarantees that no person shall be deprived of liberty without due process of law. It is the duty of the courts to vindicate those guarantees. It is vital that all their evidence be given to you well in advance of trial.

Often, a prosecutor will refuse to disclose information, hiding behind some supposed legal privilege that forbids him from doing so.

Such a privilege is based only on the generalized interest in confidentiality; it cannot win over your right to a fair trial. The generalized assertion of privilege must yield to the demonstrated, specific need for evidence in a criminal trial. To provide protection against public disclosure of the alleged privileged material, sometimes the court will conduct an inspection of the evidence *in camera* (in chambers) and determine whether it should be used at trial.

The Kingdom of Murk—Stall Until the Last Minute

**"An incompetent attorney can delay a trial for months.
A competent attorney can delay one even longer."
—EVELLE J. YOUNGER (1904-1971)**

A key element in the government's strategy is to delay the sharing of any evidence until the last possible minute. It's the prosecutor's stonewall trick.

They do not disclose any exculpatory (helpful) evidence. Anything showing that the accused did not do it, or anything that reduces punishment, is supposed to be disclosed under the U.S. Supreme Court case of *Brady v. Maryland*.

A *Brady v. Maryland* motion is like a vacuum cleaner, sucking up everything and handing it over to you. It is always granted by the judge but rarely obeyed by the prosecutor. There should be no reason to hide anything unless there is a desperate need to win—at all costs.

Government witnesses can rarely be interviewed. Prosecutors discourage them from talking to the defense lawyer, and so they seldom do.

The defense attorney is outmanned and outgunned by the resource of hundreds of police officers, deputy sheriffs, highway patrolmen, and federal agents—hardly a level playing field.

Amending Charges at the Last Minute

Sometimes it takes months, even years, for criminal cases to come to trial. Prosecuting attorneys decide on the charge they are going to file, and you are afforded the right of a preliminary hearing. Eventually you are bound over for trial on a particular charge. It is not uncommon that on the day of trial the prosecuting attorney will move to amend the criminal charge.

Courts rule that unless you can prove that you are prejudiced, the amendment to the charge should be approved. As long as it is still generally encompassed in the original statutory charge, then prejudice does not exist.

The simple truth is that many prosecutors do not seriously review the criminal charge prior to trial. As they are preparing for trial, they change the charge in order to more easily prove their case. They play keep-away with it so you may not know your exact criminal charge until the actual day of trial. Surprise!

Prosecutors' One-Way Secret Subpoenas

State prosecutors are given the right to issue *private investigative subpoenas*. These should be illegal, since they are *ex parte* (one-way) communications with a witness before criminal charges are even filed. But with no advance notice or right to object afforded to you, the target of the investigation, prosecutors get judges to issue subpoenas to make people come to their office, testify, and produce written documents.

Prosecutors can get private medical records or bank records prior to the filing of any criminal charge. Then, if they wish, they can obtain a search warrant based on the information they received from the one way subpoena. Records of these subpoenas are required to be kept in the circuit clerk's office. They never are.

Worse, the prosecutor does not need probable cause, which the Fourth Amendment seems to require. He needs only suspicion, without any explanation whatsoever as to whether the testimony or records obtained from the investigative subpoena could be relevant to some legitimate criminal investigation. He can secretly issue such subpoenas while your case is pending in court. This law should be repealed.

Badgering

The prosecuting attorney or one of his investigators may try to talk with you even after you have already employed an attorney. This is strictly unethical as our rules of ethics prohibit an opposing lawyer to communicate with you on a subject when he knows you've hired a lawyer.

Nonetheless, even though questioning is improper, if you give a statement that prosecutors deem to be inconsistent with a previous statement that you might have given, they can still use the statement against you once you testify at trial.

Loose Cannon Prosecutors

When a rogue prosecutor commits misconduct during trial but does not prejudice you so as to require reversal, there is little penalty. Courts usually warn the prosecutor or his office not to commit the misconduct again. This toothless admonition is a judicial tongue-clicking. No harm, no foul.

The absence of effective sanctions for prosecutors who engage in unethical conduct is much like the fox guarding the henhouse. There are an increasing number of "loose cannon" prosecutors who engage in outrageous conduct because they know they are essentially immune.

Personal Participation in Investigation

Prosecutors are not supposed to personally participate or be present at lineups, questioning, or search warrant raids. They will, however, on occasion accompany police because they are zealous and fascinated with the excitement. If they do, they can become an official witness at trial and, therefore, may be disqualified from further participation in your case.

The Sentencing Caper

One weary trick of the prosecuting attorney is at sentencing. If you have been found guilty or pleaded guilty, either with or without a

116

plea bargain agreement, you may think the fireworks are over. Either the prosecutor is going to recommend a particular sentence to the judge, or perhaps the Presentence Investigation Report recommends a particular sentence. You show up for court and think that it's basically over except the shouting (or moaning).

Surprise! The prosecutor shows up in court with a prepared statement. Accompanying him are police officer witnesses, the victim, and the victim's family, who are all prepared to make statements and weep and cry. It's a big show.

Because of victims' rights laws, you are required to endure your evil deeds five times (plea of guilty, presentence investigation, opening argument at sentencing, sentencing evidence, and closing argument at sentencing). The idea is to prejudice you to the judge or make a play to the news media and courtroom audience.

Office of Professional Responsibility

If you have a complaint against a U.s. Attorney, you can complain to the Office of Professional Responsibility. Forget it. It's a whitewash. The U.S. Department of Justice supposedly has internal controls on federal prosecutors regarding the disciplinary action it has taken concerning prosecutorial misconduct. Do not waste your time.

In state court, there is a secret disciplinary committee that meets behind closed doors. In fifty years, I have known few prosecutors who were disciplined, although a large number of defense lawyers have been.

"When you have no basis for argument, abuse the plaintiff."
—Cicero (106-43 b.c.)

"Foul unto others as they foul unto me."
—Shaquille O'Neal
Los Angles Lakers (2001)

Tricks Police Play

The Ten Worst Things to Say to a Police Officer:

10. I can't reach my license unless you hold my beer.
9. I thought you had to be in relatively good physical condition to be a cop.
8. You're not gonna check the trunk, are you?
7. Gee, that gut sure doesn't inspire confidence.
6. Didn't I see you get your butt kicked on Cops?
5. I pay your salary!
4. Gee, Officer! That's terrific. The last cop only gave me a warning, too!
3. I was trying to keep up with traffic. Yes, I know there is no other car around-that's how far ahead of me they are.
2. Well, when I reached down to pick up my bag of crack, my gun fell off my lap and got stuck behind the gas pedal, forcing me to speed out of control.
1. Hey, is that a nine-millimeter? That's nothing compared to this forty-four magnum.

"We got the motive, which is money. And the body, which is dead."
—ROD STEIGER (1930-2002)
In the Heat of the Night, 1968

> "Great peace have those who love your law,
> and nothing causes them to stumble."
> —PSALM 119:165

The vast majority of police officers are dedicated, honest, and hard-working, and only want to do their job. Most, because of a pure love for the job, work their entire adult lifetime at their chosen career. They are often required to work second jobs to make ends meet, and their spouses must work to provide even a basic lifestyle.

This book is not about these dedicated individuals. This book looks at the other side—the police officer who cuts corners, falsifies a police report, mishandles evidence, and believes a small lie in court is justified because it serves the greater good (in his opinion) of putting the criminal behind bars. And as we all know, such cops do exist.

This book is about millions of Americans each year who run afoul of the law. You receive a traffic ticket or something worse, and suddenly, as a law-abiding citizen, you find yourself on the receiving end. The government wants to prosecute you, give you a permanent criminal record, and send you to jail or prison.

You may be entirely innocent or you may be only partly guilty. Due to alcohol, drug use, or just plain bad judgment, you caught the eye of an arresting officer. Suddenly you are a target.

Where do you turn? What are your rights? Do you need a lawyer and if so, which one? And once you get a lawyer, can you trust him to be on your side and not sell you out?

They can easily intimidate. They are professional interrogators. They feel comfortable wearing a uniform, badge, and a service re-volver. Their presence carries the full power of the law. The problem comes from the fact that you're not sure what full power they have. You're not sure about your constitutional rights and how to exercise them. Most of all, you don't want your liberty interfered with—you don't want to go to jail. You're scared to refuse to answer questions or ask for an attorney for fear they'll think you're guilty. Not to worry—they already think you're guilty.

All your life you were told, "The policeman is your friend. If you ever need help, ask a policeman." Now the tables are turned. You're the one whose freedom is threatened because a cop thinks he has probable cause.

Foolery

"Even a fool when he holds his peace is counted wise."
—PROVERBS 17:28

"I see you're doing your Christmas shoplifting early."
—GROUCHO MARX (1890-1977)

Some people are absolute fools. How can you identify them? Look at how they think and act and look at their friends. They get into trouble and act foolishly. They don't consider the consequences of their actions.

Once the law is on to you, don't talk! The hardest thing to do is to shut up. Although you may have been a fool, perhaps the police can't prove it or they need more proof. They want you to talk and provide the necessary proof in order to convict and punish you. You are invited to hand over your head on a silver platter.

They don't have the evidence to send you to prison so they request your help. Some people have a doctorate in foolery and hone it to a science. The stupid ones commit crimes, the really stupid get caught, and the monumentally stupid attempt to match wits with a professional interrogator.

Nothing will help you. What you say will be used as they come at you from different angles. Different interrogators will question you, and for a long period of time, as long as you let them. There is no end.

Now get this straight once and for all—shut up! Get the advice of a lawyer. If you cannot reach one, then don't talk until you do.

Many police officers will violate your constitutional rights directly or sometimes indirectly or discreetly. They will tell you not to get an attorney and that attorneys are dishonest or they charge too much. They lie and claim that if you do employ an attorney, they won't talk with you and you'll go to jail. Every con imaginable can and will be used.

Police interrogation gimmicks include the following:

- "Confess, and we'll let you talk to your family."
- "God wants you to tell the truth."
- Good cop/bad cop routine.
- Disparaging your attorney; calling him names.
- "Get it off your chest. You'll feel better."
- "What will you tell your children, your family; and God?"
- The policeman is your friend. He will tell the prosecuting attorney and judge just how good you are.
- "We will do you a favor by not arresting your wife."
- "We promise not to tell your neighbors and arrest you quietly with no publicity."
- "If you talk, we promise to help get you a low bond."
- "We will let you go home tonight." (Of course, you go to prison later.)
- "If you consent to a search and show us the dope, we won't mess up your house."

Expect the police to refuse to tell you what they know. They have the right to lie and mislead you. They will not tell you who their informant is, and they never give you a photocopy of your signed statement.

Rule: **If you're one hundred percent innocent and can prove it, go ahead and talk. The truth will set you free.**

Rule: **If you're guilty, a little guilty, or have some guilty knowledge, don't talk until you've had a chance to talk to your lawyer.**

Ignore Them and They'll Go Away

**"A prudent man sees danger and takes refuge,
but the simple keep going and suffer for it."
—PROVERBS 13:16**

"When one is alone and unarmed,
a surrender may be pardoned."
—NAPOLEON BONAPARTE (1769-1821)

May a police officer approach you on the street or sidewalk, or while you are being seated on a bus, train, or plane, temporarily block your exit, stand in front of you, and question you? Unbelievably; the answer is yes!

If a policeman places you in tight quarters and you feel constrained and not free to leave, it is improper police practice. If a reasonable citizen would not feel free to leave, then it is an illegal arrest.

Speaking to someone in a conversational tone in a public place does not constitute an arrest. The increasingly common drug interdiction tactic—where police board a passenger bus during a layover without any suspicion whatsoever and request travelers' consent to search their persons or luggage—is perfectly legal.

Rule: **If police attempt to question you on the street or in your car about matters unrelated to your original stop, shut up! Do not be intimidated. Tell the officer you are leaving. Make him make the first move by detaining you. You can challenge his arrest in court and win.**

Knock and Talk

Rule: **There is nothing wrong with having nothing to say, as long as you don't say it out loud.**

If you've been snitched out by a former girlfriend or pal who's been arrested and is turning in friends to "work off' his or her troubles, be alert to an unassuming knock on the door.

- Don't open the door. Yell through the door to the cops and determine the purpose of the visit. Don't give in.
- If you do open the door, don't open the screen/glass door. Don't even touch it. Keep it closed. Once they get their foot in the

122

door, you will never get them out.

- Whatever you do, don't let the cops in. If you screw up and let them in, you'll have a devil of a time getting rid of them. Show them to the door. Get a camera to take their photo. Turn on a tape recorder and audibly tell them to leave. Cops hate cameras and tape recorders, especially when you have one and they don't.

In a knock and talk, the cops sit at your kitchen table and want you to confess to all manner of crimes, especially drug possession. They want you to roll over and play dead. Get serious. They don't have probable cause to search. Tell them to butt out and scram.

Protective Sweep

Police are allowed to search further if it's under the excuse of a protective sweep. Whether in your car, office, or home, police can make a quick cursory check for weapons. If during the process of patting you down, squeezing the outside of your suitcase, or looking into various rooms and closets of your home, evidence of another crime is discovered, you've probably had it. Police will always claim they saw things in your house in plain view during a protective sweep. You lose.

Their Word Against Yours—and You Lose!

"Depend upon it, Sir, when a man knows he is to be hanged in a fortnight, it concentrates his mind wonderfully."
—SAMUEL JOHNSON (1696-1772)

"You ain't heard nothin' yet, folks."
—AL JOLSON (1886-1950)

One of the most brazen tactics used by law enforcement officers is for two or more of them to interview you. They make their initial notes (known as field notes), return to their headquarters and write their reports, in which they can misquote you or misrepresent the facts. The original field notes are always destroyed, either thrown out in the trash or shredded. You need to get your story straight and stick with it. Concentrate your mind.

Every officer has *Miranda* warning rights papers in his briefcase (usually carried in the trunk of his patrol car or kept in his desk), but you're seldom asked to sign a written waiver of your *Miranda* rights.

Even if there are two or three officers, only one of them will do a report. That way, although they try to catch you in conflicting stories, they can't get caught in any conflicts. At trial, they will all read from one officer's report and all of them will testify the same way.

Even though this is wrong, they are not about to change since they are usually successful in setting up a "swearing match." It's you against them, and guess who the judge or jury is likely to believe?

The Old "Destruction of Notes" Trick

Most law enforcement officers will not videotape or tape record you during an interview. They really don't want your exact words quoted, especially where you question the need for an attorney, or that you want to talk to family or friends before proceeding further with the interview. They would much prefer to reduce the encounter to a situation where they are making notes of your words. Then after they've had an opportunity to do several rough drafts on their computer, they will quote you in a subsequent typed report and thereby slant or "spin" what you said or did to make it look as though you're guilty. For instance, they will note in their report that you appeared nervous when asked certain key questions, that you avoided eye contact, looked down, or buried your head in your hands when, in fact, your actions were entirely out of context.

Even though you've been interviewed for more than an hour, their one-page report will only have bits and pieces containing certain alleged incriminating statements that you've made which were totally taken out of context but placed in quotes in their report.

All the voluminous information that you have given them is omitted, not placed in their report, and simply discarded by them as nonessential.

At trial, they will be questioned about why they didn't video or tape record you. They will say it is simply not their policy, or they don't have a tape recorder, or the tape recorder was not handy, or they do not have adequate secretarial staff to type up transcripts, or they do not have room for storage of such information. There will be a dozen worthless excuses depending upon the ingenuity and the quick thinking of the officer on the witness stand.

Intimidation

"It may be true that the law cannot make a man love me, but it can keep him from lynching me, and I think that's pretty important."
—DR. MARTIN LUTHER KING, JR.
(1929-1968)

"There's no going back. A brand sticks.
You're either right or wrong. You can't break the mold."
—ALAN LADD
Shane, 1953

Police know that once you are taken into custody and are either formally arrested or handcuffed, or it is otherwise made clear to you that you are not free to leave, then you are under formal arrest. For any questioning to be legal and admissible in court, you must have been formally advised of your *Miranda* warning rights under the rule of *Miranda v. Arizona* (1964).

The trick that police play is that by their comments to others, or to you, or a wink, nod, or action, they attempt to coerce you into making statements by suggesting that things will go better if you get it off your chest. Comments like "The truth never hurts" or "It's time to come clean," or other comments that are the functional equivalent of questioning, trick you into making a statement that will haunt you at trial.

Police always testify they never said or did anything to coerce your word, that your statements were all voluntary and were not made in response to any questioning.

Look out for the good cop—bad cop routine. One cop is mean and threatening. The other one is your friend. They're masterful at this

125

gimmick.

How Police Work

"I'm not against the police; I'm just afraid of them."
—ALFRED HITCHCOCK (1899-1980)

"The true measure of justice is not how we treat our best of citizens, but how it treats those who are perceived as our worst."
—CLARENCE DARROW (1857-1938)

Police are charged with both preventing crime before it occurs and arresting those who have already broken the law. They want a free hand to search for evidence, seize contraband (guns and drugs), interrogate suspects, and have victims identify suspects.

At trial, police must provide the prosecutor with sufficient evidence to prove guilt beyond a reasonable doubt. They know they must make every effort to gather physical evidence, obtain confessions, and take witness statements to prove their case in court.

The need for police to gather evidence can conflict with the constitutional rights of citizens. Although they may want to search a home, the Fourth Amendment restricts police activities by requiring them to obtain a search warrant. Police may wish to vigorously interrogate a suspect, but they must honor the Fifth Amendment~prohibition against forcing people to incriminate themselves.

This conflict between police and the criminal suspect has been refereed by the courts. The U.S. Supreme Court has used its power to set limits on police operations, going so far as to punish them by excluding from trial any evidence obtained in violation of a suspect's constitutional rights (the Exclusionary Rule).

Once a crime has been committed, police use various methods to collect evidence needed for criminal prosecution. With each crime, police must decide how best to investigate, which includes the following:

1. Engaging in surveillance of your home or business to acquire additional evidence and to discourage any criminal activity;

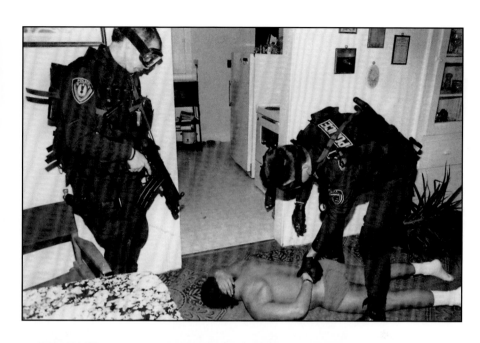

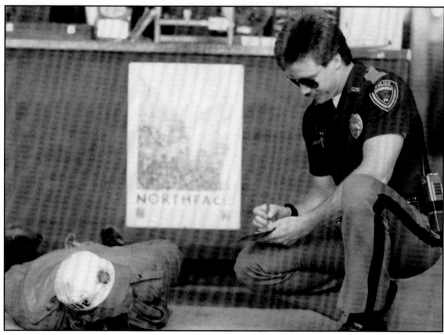

What it feels like.

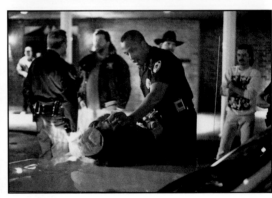

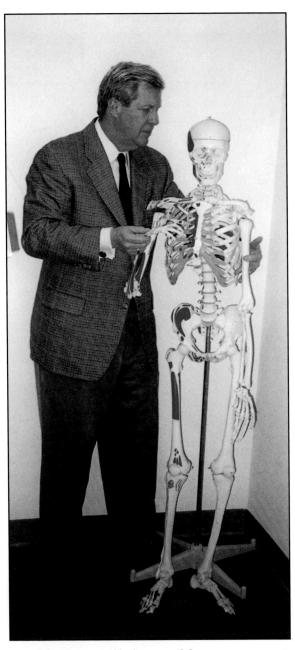

A good lawyer will thoroughly cross-examine
and pick apart a hostile witness.

Your lawyer will advise you on whether you should testify in your own defense - but you will make the final decision.

SARASOTA COUNTY

PAUL REUBENS
Indecent exposure

139813
C LEVELAND
32 5 8 128
NOV 3 1970

JANE FONDA
Drug smuggling, assault and battery of a police officer

DEC 20 971

LARRY KING
Scamming a business associate out of $5,000

BK 4013970 081794

O.J. SIMPSON
Double homicide with "special circumstances"

ID NO. DATE
974254 05:27:97

MARV ALBERT
Assault and battery

BK 4059869 07 26 94
LOS ANGELES POLICE NWD

MICKEY ROURKE
Spousal abuse

BK 5907092 03 21 94
LOS ANGELES POLICE PAC

DUDLEY MOORE
Cohabitational abuse

GREENWOOD LAKE
POLICE DEPT
GL 1027
5-12-69

LINDA TRIPP
Loitering

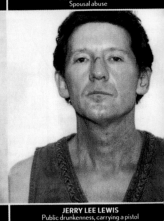

JERRY LEE LEWIS
Public drunkenness, carrying a pistol

KEANU REEVES
Drunk driving and struggling with the police

SUZANNE SOMERS
Paying rent with a bad check

TIM ALLEN
Possession and distribution of narcotics

HOMER D. WAMPLER, III
Attorney

Wampler later escapes from jail

BRETT BUTLER
Drunk driving

ANNA NICOLE SMITH
Driving while intoxicated

WOODY HARRELSON
Disorderly conduct

AL PACINO
Carrying a concealed weapon in a motor vehicle

▲ JULY 4 **After the incident, Bryant goes home to California but returns to Colorado two days later for a booking**

Nick Nolte's mug shot taken after police California stopped his swerving car.

Sheen initially faced a court in June 1997 after entering a plea of no contest to assault charges by then-girlfriend Brittany Ashland. Below: A year later, on Aug. 10, 1998, he leaves the courthouse after a judge forces him to choose between jail or drug treatment.

2. Searching persons or vehicles;
3. Confiscating illegal drugs, guns, or money either in connection with the arrest or to remove them from circulation;
4. Trading immunity from arrest for information or cooperation;
5. Detaining persons temporarily for purposes other than prosecution, such as further investigation, safekeeping, or simple harassment;
6. Recruiting snitches;
7. Interviewing your neighbors;
8. Aerial flyovers and photographs;
9. Tape-recording you on the telephone;
10. Inspecting your trash; and
11. Knocking on your door for plain view or plain smell.

Judges take an active role in considering the legality of police work and trying to stop police from violating a person's constitutional rights. They are moderately successful—some judges more than others.

> **"I ought to bust your butt down to Traffic, or better yet, kick it off the force. You're a dinosaur, Callahan. Your ideas don't fit today."**
> —BRADFORD DILLMAN as Captain Briggs to Inspector Harry Callahan (Clint Eastwood) in *Sudden Impact* (1983)

Big Brother Is Watching You

U.S. spy satellites have been peeking at you since the 1970s, but their capabilities are the stuff of science fiction. Global coverage, resolution to ten centimeters, and radar imaging that peers through are now possible. Private satellites (Ikonons) provide images with resolution down to thirty-two inches. Forward Looking Infrared (FUR) cameras can see through walls. Police stations nationwide already have helicopters outfitted with these gadgets. They detect heat sources, such as grow lamps used for cultivating pot. They can spot a man running through a forest at night from hundreds of yards or pick out a car that recently had its engine on.

Snooper Technology

In 2001, the U.S. Supreme Court (*Kallo v. U.S.*) refused to allow infrared technology to pry into a home and spot excess heat coming off high-intensity grow lights, ruling that police were conducting an unconstitutional search.

"Off-the-wall" technologies like infrared guns—which can pick up signals only from the outside of a building—are legal, but "through-the-wall" devices that can see inside are illegal.

There is a whole new generation of surveillance technology springing up at airports, prisons, border crossings, and crime scenes. Although they're not up to the standards of Superman, they can see through clothing and peer into private homes well enough to raise thorny privacy issues for all of us:

- *X-ray vision.* X-ray devices are today's preferred technology for looking through things. The U.S. Customs Service recently placed an order for thousands of X-ray inspection systems. Images are made from X-rays, scattered back from objects (rather than passing through them) with extraordinary clarity. Guns, drugs, plastic explosives, and other contraband can be seen even when hidden in the middle of a fully packed eighteen-wheeler. One product (called Body-Search) reveals ghostly images of weapons and whatever else—including genitals—that may be hidden underneath your clothes.
- *Radar Flashlights.* A radar flashlight looks like an oversized hair dryer, but, it can penetrate an eight-inch-thick nonmetal door or wall. While radar waves encounter moving objects, like a hostage-taker's nervous pacing, the motions are translated into a bar of LED lights. The height of the bar corresponds with the amount of movement in the room. In radar detectors, the crude LED display is replaced by dancing circles and colored blobs that show both the location and trajectory of moving objects on the other side of a wall or barrier.
- *Beyond Bar Graphs.* Using shorter radar waves measured in

millimeters, not centimeters, a device can go well beyond colored blobs. The human body naturally emits short-wavelength
radiation that goes right through clothes. Anything blocking
that emission, such as a concealed gun or wallet, shows up as
a shadow.

There should be a law blocking the use of future imaging technologies to peer in your home where you have a reasonable expectation of privacy.

Police have two outs:

1. Why don't they get a search warrant? If cops have good reason
   to peer inside your house, they can always go to a judge and get
   advance permission—just as they do today with a wiretap. Ever
   heard of the Sixth Amendment?
2. Or police can wait for technology to become more commonly
   used. If everybody owns a through-the-wall imager, then nobody can reasonably expect any privacy anywhere, even at
   home.

Big Brother's Neighbors

Slowly but surely, we've become a nation of stool pigeons. Agencies at all levels have buckets of money to throw at people who squeal.
Government -sponsored snitching has increased across the country.
Programs pay Medicare recipients a thousand dollars to inform on
their doctors, and students receive cash for reporting smoking, drinking, and drug violations by their classmates. A county government in
Virginia even pays homeowners to report neighbors with cluttered
lawns.

The number of federal search warrants relying exclusively on uni-
dentified informants is well over seventy percent. Federal money is
paid to report realtors, banks, and landlords for violating fair housing
laws. The real kings of this technique are the folks at the IRS who pay
informants up to fifteen percent of the taxes recovered as a result of
the tips—to a maximum reward of two million dollars.

The Spying Game

Today the U.S. government runs the most powerful surveillance network the world has ever known. Spies use programs like Echelon and Carnivore to listen to your phone signals from space and monitor your Web surfing, compelling your own service providers to betray you. Privacy in America will soon become nothing more than a fond memory.

The FBI surveillance tool called Carnivore investigates people who may be using the Internet to commit crimes. The FBI targets the ISP and hooks up a back door to a government computer, which scans information passing to the ISP's network. It searches only the sender and recipient line of e-mails, not the subject or message itself, according to the Feds—if you trust the Feds. It has the power to analyze millions of messages per second, accessing all information about every customer of an Internet service provider (ISP).

One-third of all U.S. employees are monitored by their bosses when they go online. Private industry has gotten into the act and commercial snooping has exploded. It's not only "You've got mail," but also "You've got company."

The system called Echelon intercepts up to three billion satellite communications every day. If you make an international call, there's a ninety percent chance Echelon is recording you. Agents identify the phone number, use voice recognition software to spot targets, and tag conversations with a computer called "Dictionary."

There are a dozen oversight committees in Congress and the executive branch, but there's no way to know whether the agency is obeying the law.

When technologies converge, it should be very scary. Cell phones became common just as the Internet spread worldwide, and the two have now partnered up. Yahoo! News headlines are available to anyone with a mobile phone.

What will happen when surveillance technologies merge? When facial recognition is connected to holographic storage systems with national DMV records? When private satellites transmit high-resolution infrared photos to anyone who pays for them?

Privacy-sapping technology is developing every day, and state and federal agencies—not to mention all kinds of private organizations—are constantly finding new ways to use and abuse it. At the current rate of apathy and growing government power, privacy is a goner—or perhaps it's already vanished.

Digital Spies Watch Your Keystrokes

There are various high-tech "check-you-at-the-door" spying systems designed to stop store employees from pilfering, to impose chilling and insane degrees of electronic supervision, or to conduct keystroke-by-keystroke surveillance. Some applications are ridiculous and counterproductive, but nonetheless, employers have the right to use them.

Powerful people are preoccupied with getting other people to work harder, and of course, stopping embezzlement and pilfering is a good cause.

Eighty percent of all U.S. corporations—including retail stores, restaurants, trucking firms, and hospitals—now keep employees under regular surveillance by computer. They do not have to notify employees that they are being snooped upon.

The pressure to ratchet up performance is endless. E-mail, telephone calls, computer files, Internet logs, even keystrokes—are all monitored. Telecommuters and business travelers are included.

Technological changes are coming thick and fast. The Federal Trade Commission is looking for more authority to enforce privacy issues. In the meantime, you have two choices: you can raise hell or you can quit your job.

Internet Insecurity

Today with commercial spyware, which can be downloaded free, you can rifle through another person's hard drive, control his computer, and surf the Web.

Obtaining another person's Social Security number is a key to the kingdom. You can get a driver's license, start full-scale identity theft, ruin a credit rating, drain a bank account—you get the idea. You have zero privacy on the Internet, so get over it.

Certain operating systems have a serious vulnerability that lets hackers take control:

- Someone might use the Internet to steal your identity.
- You may be intentionally revealing information about yourself as you move through cyberspace.
- That personal information you have just provided to a Web site might be sold or stolen.
- The Web site on which you just entered your credit card number may be fake.
- The government may be giving out your home address, Social Security number, and other personal information online.
- For-profit companies and people who don't like you may be broadcasting your private information on the Internet.
- Your company, your spouse, or a stranger may be using your computer to spy on you.
- Beware the Cybercops.
- Our desire to ever tighten the boundaries of our nation, with increased surveillance and suspicion within, is directly related to terrorist attacks. We should resist the notion that heightened scrutiny, especially if inconspicuous to the public, carries no significant cost to law-abiding citizens.
- Internet monitoring is unnoticeable as we surf.
- Informally calling it the "return of the lock box," our government asked for massive government data vaults, routinely receiving copies of all internet traffic—emails, web pages, chats, mouse clicks, shopping, pirated music—for later retrieval should the government decide it needs more information to

solve some crime.
- After September 11, 2001, we should not be lulled into a sense that civil liberties are dispensable luxuries. Of course, we have legitimate fright but lock boxes holding our expressions, thoughts, and ideals should not be surveilled and invaded.
- Three ways to more secure cyber safety include:
  1. Install a home firewall and virus protection.
  2. Be careful what you give out.
  3. Don't download anything unless you trust the symbol and the file.

How to Talk to a Detective

"The check is in the mail."
"Of course I'll respect you tomorrow."
"I'm from the government and I'm here to help you."
—WORLD'S BIGGEST LIES

"There are men in all ages who mean to govern well, but they mean to govern. They promise to be good masters, but they mean to be masters."
—DANIEL WEBSTER (1782-1852)

"Women are like the police. They could have all the evidence in the world, but they still want the confession."
—CHRIS ROCK

You should take great care if you are approached by a police detective or investigator from a federal agency, such as the IRS, FBI, or DEA.

How do you talk to a cop? Very carefully! If you are a hundred percent innocent, with no guilty knowledge of the crime, talk. If you are in any way knowledgeable of a crime, say nothing. Assert your right to an attorney before you make any comments.

1. They will surprise you.

- They will never call for an appointment. The surprise is an advantage to them, catching you off guard and unaware. Your mind is on other things. Suddenly, two friendly men politely request a few minutes of your time, showing you an important-looking badge.
- You are embarrassed, frightened, and yet honored that someone so important would want a few minutes of your time. Demand to see their identification and get their personal business cards.
2. They will be polite, low-key, and businesslike.
   - Detectives are not mean or antagonistic. They will be conservatively well dressed, will identify themselves, and will get to the point. They may smile or chat to disarm you or gain your confidence—they look friendly enough. They will request a private room where they can talk to you alone or try to gain admittance to your house. You are hoping they will go away if you give the right answers. They will take brief notes but not tape-record you, since they would have to give the tape to your lawyer. Later, when they testify against you at trial, they can misquote you, and it is their word against yours as to what was said. You lose.
3. They will convince you it's in your best interest to talk.
   - They begin low-key and work their way up. They only want a few minutes and have only a few questions.
   - Once the cat is out of the bag and you have established a friendly attitude and begin to answer their questions, you're hooked! They'll take longer than a few minutes; ask pointed, planned questions; and watch your mannerisms and body language. They'll sense whether you are lying or uncomfortable as you talk, and you will become increasingly uncomfortable.
   - Once you start talking, it is hard to stop and request a lawyer, get them out of your house, or walk away. You'll appear guilty or unfriendly if you demand your constitutional rights. They may not advise you of your *Miranda* warning rights (they're not required to, since you are not in custody).
   - Demand to know pointedly: "Do you have a grand jury subpoena in your pocket?" Place the burden on them.

- Detectives are information-gathering experts. They listen to your answers and gather information. They do not give out information. The surest way to counter a detective is to ask for information:
  - "What is your purpose in being here?"
  - "Am I under a grand jury investigation?"
  - "Am I under investigation by your agency?"
  - "Who sent you here?"
  - "Why didn't you call me for an appointment?"
  - "What specific crimes do you believe I have committed?"
  - "Who told you that?"
  - "Do you already have a subpoena for me?"
  - "Am I a target?"
  - "Are you giving me full immunity?"
  - "Will you please write out your questions and my lawyer will answer them."

- They will beat around the bush without giving you a direct answer, and you will learn little more than vague generalities.
4. They will take no written or tape-recorded statement from you.
  - At trial, they will establish a two-to-one ratio against you. They will not permit anyone else to be present in the room who might act as your witness. If you do decide to talk to them, assert your right to have a friend or relative present. If they refuse, you should leave.
  - When dealing with a detective, turn on a tape recorder and record the entire conversation. Ask them questions and soon they will leave.

Rules When Agents Approach You

1. Don't move. If they were rude enough to come unannounced to your home or business, make them talk to you in front of others. They will be uncomfortable because they don't like neutral witnesses.
2. Don't make an appointment or agree to see them later. You are only inviting trouble.

3. Don't give them any documentary evidence or sign any statements. Demand that you be given a photocopy of the evidence or an immediate carbon copy. They won't like this and will refuse.

4. Demand their personal business cards. Since you are nervous, you will want their full names to give to your attorney.

5. When asked to talk, tell them you'll be glad to talk in the presence of your attorney. Answer nothing further. They have no right to ask the name of your attorney or question you further. The law prohibits them from badgering you.

6. Be firm! If they pester, beg, badger, or intimidate, get mean! If they refuse to leave, threaten to call the police and prosecute them for trespassing. Don't worry about making them mad. They already believe you're guilty.

7. After you talk with your attorney, reflect on your predicament. Then and only then, if you want to talk, you may do so. Your previous refusal to talk cannot ever be used against you or mentioned in court.

8. Do not let them in your house! Do not open the screen door. Talk through the door. If they get into your living room, tell them to leave. If they refuse, then you leave.

9. If they contact you at work and speak loudly to embarrass you, tell them to leave. Show them the door. It will exasperate them.

Detectives go to work each day for one purpose: To detect, investigate, arrest, and convict people they perceive as guilty. At the time they're talking to you, this means you! They're satisfied when people are convicted and go to prison. This is their job. If you believe you can give them a snow job and they'll go away, you are extremely naive. You'll pay for it later.

So You've Been Stopped

Rule: **Only some of us learn by other people's mistakes; the rest of us have to be the other people.**

If you're pulled over in your car, sit perfectly still with your hands on the wheel. Don't reach for your wallet or into the glove compartment.

Wait for the police to approach you. Be polite and courteous. If you have friends in high places, don't mention it. Don't threaten or bluster. Only jerks threaten a cop. If you come on too strong, you'll get a handful of tickets instead of one.

Police can be very creative. They can and will cite you for anything from failing to signal a lane change, to a cracked windshield, to failure to have a light bulb over your license plate. Although you should freely offer your name and address, say nothing of any illegal drugs or volunteer anything until you speak with your lawyer.

The key is truthfulness. The police are experts at detecting bull. Never try to buy your way out of a ticket. You're unlikely to bribe the officer, and you'll risk being charged with attempted bribery.

Can police officers be held accountable for their actions? Yes, they can, once the incident is over. Do this discreetly and don't ask for a badge number if you don't have to. Police will construe this as a challenge. After your case is over, make a complaint to Internal Affairs.

Never plead guilty to a traffic ticket without first getting advice from a lawyer. He may help you avoid a criminal record or points on your license. It's the best money you'll ever spend. Even an incompetent lawyer can do you some good.

Talking Your Way Out of a Traffic Ticket

"Take care that thou art made into Caesar . . . keep thyself simple, good, pure, serious ... a friend of justice.
—MARCUS AURELIUS (121-180 A.D.)

When the policeman approaches you from his car, what is your frame of mind?
- It could be anger if you're in a hurry and don't want to be delayed.
- It could be indignity if you feel you've done nothing wrong.
- It could be fear if you've never been stopped before and don't know what to expect.
- It could be apathy if you really don't care.
- It could be contempt if this is the tenth time you've been stopped.

- It could be total surprise if you think you've done nothing wrong.

The responsibility for maintaining a good attitude is on you! Depending on the officer's personality and frame of mind, if there is a way to talk your way out of a ticket, it depends totally on your attitude. Keep your composure, be friendly and polite, and convey to the officer the following:

"I'm not sure if I know exactly what I've done wrong, but I know you have a good reason for stopping me. I'm at your mercy. Are you willing to discuss the situation for a moment?"

Do's:
1. Pull over as soon as possible when you see the red lights. Cooperation is essential.
2. Roll your window down, and turn your ignition and radio off.
3. Keep your driver's license and proof of insurance easily accessible.
4. Stay in your car unless the officer asks you to step out. Police prefer that you remain in the vehicle as it is safe for everyone.
5. Keep your hands where the officer can see them at all times! He becomes nervous if he can't see your hands.
6. Be cool, calm, collected, and always polite.
7. Politely inquire why you were stopped. "Have I done something wrong, Officer?" or "I'm sorry, I didn't realize I was going that fast. I guess my mind was on where I was going. Will you excuse me this time?"

It's better to ask innocent questions than make a specific statement:
- "How can I fix my car so that it will be legal?"
- "I'm normally a very safe driver, but for a second my attention was elsewhere. I promise to do better."
- "Car insurance for a person my age is quite high, so I've been trying to keep my record clean. Can you trust me not to make the same mistake again?"
- "I have a perfect driving record. If you will give me a warning this time, I'll do my best to keep it that way."
- "I know this is my fault. Can you excuse me this time? I prom-

ise you won't have to stop me again."
- "It's been a long drive. You've just made me realize I need to stop and get some coffee."
- "I'm sorry. I should be paying closer attention. My boyfriend just broke up with me and it's hard to concentrate. I promise to be more careful."
- "Officer, is there something I can do or say that will influence your decision not to write a ticket this time and give me a warning?"
- "I'm new to this area. I guess I need to pay closer attention to my driving."

Rule: If you lie, rationalize, become sarcastic, or in any way insinuate that the officer is lying, you will probably get a ticket. The less you say, the better.

DON'TS:

1. Don't hand the officer your wallet. He does not wish to be accused of stealing money.
2. Don't ever say, "You can't write me a ticket. I haven't done anything wrong."
3. Never say, "I've had five tickets. If you write me one more, I'll lose my license."
4. Even if you intend to take the matter to court, never tell the officer. He will remember your name and be better prepared to beat you by taking good notes. If you graciously accept the ticket, he may forget you.
5. Don't beg to be let off. It will probably cause the officer to want to write you a ticket even more.
6. Never make threats such as "I'll see you in court," or "I'll get your wife and kids," or "I'll get you off duty." Threats never work plus new criminal charges may be filed against you.
7. Never refuse to sign a ticket. You're not admitting guilt, only promising to appear in court. If you refuse to sign the ticket, the officer .can take you to jail and make you post bond.
8. Never argue about the violation. It's alright to tell your side of the story; but don't argue.

9. Don't try to use titles or drop names. If you're close friends with a congressman, lawyer, or mayor, it probably will not influence the officer.

Rule: **If you do get ticketed, don't forget to show up in court or clear the ticket through the mail. If you fail to do so, a warrant will be issued for your arrest.**

Fighting a Traffic Ticket

Can you fight a traffic ticket, and what are your options? The fact is you can win—the odds are in your favor. After all, you are innocent until proven guilty.

Yet about ninety percent of all Americans obediently mail in their fines, unaware of what their contributions are promoting. A few choose a better alternative—taking a stand and fighting their tickets. Studies show that of all the people who challenge citations, about fifty percent win.

The trouble is that most people don't realize how much they really end up paying for a ticket in the long run. They're intimidated by police and even more by the court system. They don't know where to start or don't want to face the humiliation of going to court and being made to look like a fool.

Where the Heck Did He Come From?

Pay attention. You have mirrors and windows in your car for a reason. Use them. If you're driving in a manner that might cause you to get a ticket, you should definitely be watching for cops. They play hide and seek, descending from overpasses onto on-ramps and merging into traffic in a move known as the "swoop maneuver." Be weary of zipping by a pack of cars in front of you. They may be going slow because there is a patrol car in front of them.

Always pass large trucks with caution because you can't see what's in front of them until you pass. Cops know this and like to hide there. Watch for cops on freeways that have crossable center dividers. They sit in the middle and wait for you to go flying by. On city streets, be careful of hospital and school zones. Many cops sit and eat lunch in front of these zones because the speed limit is usually 25 mph or lower. Be careful going around blind corners and at four-way stops.

Pay attention to what you're doing and keep your eyes open. The object is to spot them before they spot you ..

When You're Pulled Over

1. Keep your hands on the steering wheel so the officer can see them. Wait until he reaches your window and asks you for your license and registration before you make any movement. A "routine" traffic stop is always potentially dangerous for an officer.
2. Let the officer do the talking. When you answer his questions, make your replies brief and nonincriminating. When you're pulled over for speeding, the officer asks you how fast you were going. Your reply should be, "You know, I'm not really sure," or "Gosh, 1 really don't know," or "I was going with the flow of traffic."
3. The cop may ask, "Mind if I look around?" Politely tell him no. He cannot do so without probable cause or your permission. He doesn't have probable cause unless he saw you stuffing something under the seat as he approached your car or your breath smells like weed or booze.
4. If he says he can get a warrant, invite him to go ahead. The judge won't let him have a warrant since he does not have probable cause.
5. After the officer has given you a ticket and retreated to his car, give him time to pull out first. Although he is not likely to give you separate tickets in a row, it is always safer to have a cop in front of you than behind.

Radar

Of all the moving violations that are issued, the majority are speeding tickets. Everyone thinks radar is infallible because it is digital and computerized. Nothing could be further from the truth. Many factors can cause a radar reading to be inaccurate, and if you can prove or even raise a suspicion that any of these factors were involved, you have a good chance of getting your ticket dismissed.

1. The radar unit must be pointed straight at you to read your speed. There may be obstructions in the way.
2. The unit must be fairly close to you to ensure that it is not reading another vehicle in another lane. The margin of error increases with the length of the radar beam.
3. Radar can be affected by rain and blowing objects because it measures the speed of anything that moves. Blowing dust, leaves, or branches can be mistaken for your car.
4. Handheld radar guns are a problem. When the officer raises the gun quickly, the unit not only measures your speed but adds the speed of the officer's arm motion, which can be up to 8 to 10 mph. An officer's arm speed might be grounds for a speeding ticket being dismissed.
5. In some places, a police officer cannot use radar to enforce posted speed limits unless a Traffic and Engineering Survey has been conducted and maintained on that particular road. It is from these surveys that most posted speed limits are supposed to be set. They must be updated every few years for radar to be legally used.

There are other methods an officer can use to determine your speed:

- *Pacing.* If an officer follows you for a while, traveling at the same speed you are, he can pace you for a quarter of a mile. You can ask the officer the last time his speedometer was calibrated and try to obtain his calibration records before you go to court.
- *VASCAR.* Using the VASCAR (Visual Average Speed Computer and Recorder) method, an officer measures the time it takes for you to travel a known distance between two points. When you cross the beginning point, the cop starts a stopwatch. When you reach the ending point, the officer stops his watch and enters your time in a computer, which tells him how fast you were going. VASCAR is a "speed trap" but is an accurate method of determining speed as long as the officer doesn't make a mistake

or cheat.

- *Air Patrolling.* Have you ever seen one of those "Patrolled by Aircraft" signs? They're not kidding. These air patrolman use the VASCAR method for determining speed. They clock you crossing across two painted blocks on the highway and radio down to a patrolman on the ground with a description of the offending vehicle.

How to Avoid a Speeding Ticket

1. *Drive in the middle lane.* Radar guns have a difficult time gauging your speed whenever you're coasting between two cars. Avoid the left lane at all costs.
2. *Don't be fooled by cops who are already pulled over with lights flashing.* When you speed by, assuming they've already stopped someone else, they may be ready to chase you down.
3. *Beware of exit ramps, overhead passes, and parking lots.* That's where cops usually hide.

Don't Run from the Cops

"Can't we all just get along?"
—RODNEY KING (1992)

Anyone who has spent any amount of time with a police officer knows that a cop dreads having to pull the trigger.

I have spent hundreds of hours riding with uniformed and undercover officers and have a good sense of what makes these brave men and women tick. They most certainly are not motivated by a desire to run up to an unarmed man and shoot him.

During my ride-alongs with police, in virtually every situation where a cop had to chase down a fleeing suspect, the bad guy always got smacked around in the end. Their reports invariably read: "Reasonable force was used to subdue the subject," or "While we were handcuffing the subject, he slipped and fell."

It's an inevitable part of human nature. The adrenaline is flowing, emotions are raw and charged, and a police officer becomes very,

very angry when having to chase someone. None of this is an excuse or justification for a cop shooting any unarmed man, but no one will ever get shot by a police officer while being cooperative.

Whether you are being chased by a police officer or are the victim of an armed robbery, always remember the following rule.

Rule: **Never argue with a gun.**

Red Light Cameras

Red light cameras are increasingly being used to catch drivers who run red lights. This is an inexpensive way to enforce traffic laws and raise revenues. The Federal Highway Administration has approved cameras now in use throughout most of the United States.

The camera is connected to sensors called "loops," which are buried in the road at a given intersection. The system monitors the signal continuously and is triggered by any car that passes over the sensors at a predetermined minimum speed and at a specified time after the light turns red. The camera takes a second picture of the vehicle at the intersection, recording the date, time of day; and time elapsed since the light turned red. The system works under all weather conditions. The police department then sends a ticket.

In some states, the camera takes a picture of the vehicle's license plate and matches it to the registered owner. The registered owner can be held responsible for a violation regardless of who was driving at the time. In other states, the camera takes a picture of the driver.

In certain states, an owner can avoid the citation by filing a sworn affidavit saying he wasn't driving the car.

Defense

The more fingers you can get into the pie in terms of the chain of evidence, the more likely the prosecutor is going to have a problem proving his case. Your lawyer must check to see that the regulations are complied with, as there are many possible errors in the red light camera system. The device could mistakenly think the light was red when it was actually yellow if the receptors were too close and not insulated properly.

Pursuing one of these cases can be expensive because it requires experts to explain the problems with the technology.

> **"I may be ignorant, but I am not stupid."**
> —LORETTA LYNN (1942-)

Where Police Are Permitted to Make Arrests

Where the police are allowed to arrest, you may depend on whether the police have a warrant for your arrest. The police make most arrests without a warrant. If you commit a misdemeanor in the officer's presence, he is permitted to arrest you without a warrant. If the officer has probable cause (the minimum level of evidence needed to make a lawful arrest) to believe that you committed a felony, he is allowed to arrest you without a warrant, even if he did not see you commit the crime. The law permits warrantless arrests in public places, such as a street or restaurant.

To arrest you in a private place—your home or business—police must have a warrant or your consent unless there are exigent circumstances. There are two types of warrants: an arrest warrant and a search warrant. To arrest you in your own home, police must have an arrest warrant. However, if they lack a warrant but have probable

DEFENDING YOURSELF AGAINST COPS IN MISSOURI

cause for a warrantless arrest, they are permitted to put your home under surveillance, wait until you leave your home, and arrest you in a public place. Wherever you are arrested, go peacefully—and keep quiet. You can argue your case later and it is of no value to complain to the cop. Call your lawyer or bondsman.

Rules:
—If you are clearly innocent, and it is a case of mistaken identity, you should cooperate with the police and give a full and complete statement as early as possible.
—If you are guilty or have guilty knowledge of a crime for which you have been arrested, invoke your right to counsel. Demand to see an attorney before being questioned further.
—Do not ever resist the exercise of lawful authority. Even if you are opposed to the police officers' actions, go ahead and consent to their authority.
—Be careful about discussing your case with friends, neighbors, and cellmates. Anything you say can and will be used against you if they are subpoenaed to court.

The Miranda Rule

Miranda warnings are required because of a U.S. Supreme Court case called *Miranda v. Arizona.* When you are in custody, some version of the *Miranda* rights must be read to you before questioning:

1. You have the right to remain silent.
2. Anything you say can and will be used as evidence against you in a court of law.
3. You are entitled to consult with an attorney before interrogation and have an attorney present at the time of interrogation.
4. If you cannot afford an attorney, one will be appointed for you prior to any questioning if you so desire.
5. Do you understand these rights?
6. Do you wish to waive your rights and talk with me?

Police often slip up on steps 5 and 6. The *Miranda* rule was developed to protect your Fifth Amendment right against self-incrimination. Many people feel obligated to respond to police questioning. The *Miranda* warning ensures that people in custody realize that they do not have to talk to the police and have the right to the presence of an attorney.

If the *Miranda* warning is not given before questioning, or if police continue to question you after you indicate in any manner a desire to consult with an attorney before speaking, your statements as the suspect generally are inadmissible. However, it may be difficult for your attorney to suppress your statement or confession in court.

Arrest

"You get farther with a gun and a kind word than you can get with just a kind word."
—AL CAPONE (1899-1947)

Charles Moore/Black Star

The Fourth Amendment requires that all arrests, searches, and seizures be reasonable.

An arrest is the taking of a person into custody to answer for a crime and involves three elements: authority to arrest; the assertion of that authority with intention to arrest; and restraint of the person arrested. An arrest need not be made with a written arrest warrant but may be made on probable cause that a crime has been or is being committed, so long as your liberty is restrained and you are not free to leave.

Delayed Arrest

A delayed arrest is permitted. Police may back off and let you incriminate yourself, such as when a conversation is being taped. There is no duty to immediately arrest as soon as probable cause is apparent. The officer can wait, giving you more rope to hang yourself. There is no such thing as a right to a speedy arrest.

Summons

A summons is a substitute for arrest. It's a mandatory invitation to appear at a stated time and place to answer to a criminal charge.

If you refuse to sign a traffic ticket promising to voluntarily appear in court, you can be taken to jail. You'll be arraigned and bail will be set. Always sign the traffic ticket. It's no big deal.

Arrest Warrant

Missouri requires a judge's finding of probable cause before the initial issuance of a felony arrest warrant on probable cause. This is a somewhat pointless law and rarely protects a citizen from an illegal charge. Check the court docket sheet to see if there was a probable cause finding. It's a useful loophole but has no real importance, since judges rubber-stamp their docket sheets.

Sufficient information is presented to the judge so that he knows the charges are not capricious. Formal rules of evidence do not apply; the cop relies on hearsay information.

Rule: **In practice, the judge or his clerk reviews the prosecutor's proposed criminal charge and uses a rubber stamp to recite that probable cause has be~n determined to exist. A warrant is then delivered to the sheriff or police who arrive at your front door. You are transported to jail without passing Go.**

Physical Force

An arrest does not require actual physical force, touching of your body, or even formal declaration of arrest. It is sufficient if you understand that you're arrested and submit.

Police may use whatever force is believed reasonably necessary. Missouri allows the use of deadly force in felony arrests. It is also permitted especially if you are attempting to escape by use of a deadly weapon, a life is endangered, or serious injury may be inflicted-unless, of course, you're arrested without delay.

An arrest occurs by touch of the hand, tapping the shoulder, or mere gesture, as long as the officer can reasonably expect from his conduct that you believe yourself to be under arrest.

The arrest is made when you submit to the custody of the officer. The controlling fact is *substantial interference with your will to move for any appreciable time.* This is the *free to leave test.* If you do not feel free to leave, then you are, in effect, under arrest.

If cops are playing games with you—blocking your exit or accusing you—call their bluff. Try to leave. Tell them you feel restrained. Make them make a move and either arrest you or let you go. Whatever you do, shut up!

Using Discretion in Deciding Not to Arrest

In many situations, good police practice requires no formal arrest. Such situations include minor traffic offenses, situations where an arrest might cause a disturbance or riot, minor domestic disputes, or helping an intoxicated person get home if he is creating no danger to the public.

The policeman's primary job is to protect the public. When an arrest might cause greater risk or harm to the public, or merely embarrass a person posing no real threat to the community, proper police practice may call for a decision not to arrest.

Such occurrences call for using good judgment or are controlled by local departmental policy. Not all situations in which an arrest may be made are situations in which an arrest *should* be made.

Hot Pursuit

If you are stupid enough to run from the police, you can be pursued across city; county; or state lines. *Hot pursuit* is the immediate chase of a person fleeing to avoid arrest.

This doctrine also applies if you are standing in the doorway of your home or front yard. and run into the house to hide. The fact that hot pursuit may end almost as soon as it begins does not make it any less a hot pursuit, sufficient to justify the warrantless entry into the house.

Probable Cause

For an arrest or search to be legal, it must have been based upon *probable cause.* Courts speak of *probable cause, reasonable grounds,* and *reasonable cause,* but all are treated the same and become the crucial issue in a pretrial suppression hearing.

An arrest is illegal if not based upon probable cause. Information obtained as a result of an illegal arrest is also illegal and inadmissible in court. Under the exclusionary rule, a defense attorney can file a pretrial motion to suppress the incriminating evidence and have it declared illegal.

Anonymous Tipsters

If an anonymous informant calls police and provides information on you, the report is deemed reliable if the police believe they have reasonably trustworthy information sufficient to warrant a prudent man to believe a crime is being committed.

Courts use the *whole picture test* or *totality of circumstances test* to determine the reliability of the citizen's information:

1. Whether the informant was exposed to possible criminal or civil prosecution if the report was false;
2. Whether the report was based on personal observation; and
3. Whether the officer's personal observation corroborates the informant's observation.

If a court believes that the informant's tip carries sufficient reliability, it will justify an investigative stop from which police develop probable cause sufficient to support an arrest or search warrant.

Anonymous telephone calls to police provide sufficient justification for police to start investigations, but the tip itself probably will not justify a warrantless arrest or search.

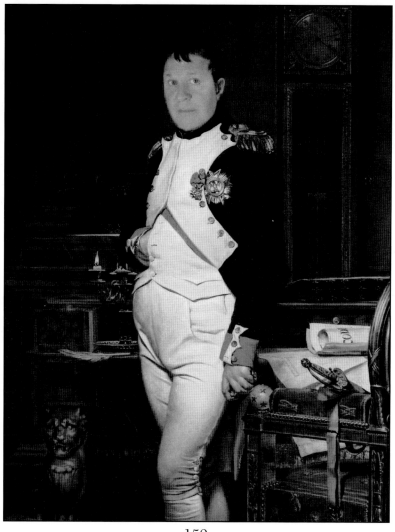

Dee-Fense!

"I'm going to fight hard. I'm going to give them hell."
—HARRY S. TRUMAN (1884-1972)

"Attack when they are unprepared, make your move when they
do not expect it."
—SUN TZU (544-496 B.C.)
The Art of War

"I think they have some 'splaining to do."
—DESI ARNAZ (1917-1986)
as Ricky Ricardo,
I Love Lucy

There are a large number of defenses available in a criminal trial.
Your defense depends upon both the facts in your case and the
truth of what actually happened.

One of the first decisions in defending yourself is to decide whether to defend on the facts or the law:

- *Facts.* If there is a factual dispute as to whether you were present or have an alibi, whether the contraband was in fact stolen
  or amounted to more than $750, or whether the eyewitness is
  correct in his identification or could be mistaken, then such a
  case needs to be tried before a jury. The jury is the great fact

finder and will determine beyond a reasonable doubt whether the prosecution witnesses should be believed. Cases involving factual disputes are best resolved by a jury!

- *Law.* If you defend on legal grounds, you should go to trial before the judge sitting alone without a jury (bench trial). If you have filed a motion to suppress the warrantless search of your home, or contest the validity of a search warrant, or contest whether *Miranda* warnings were legally given, a judge can best determine these legal questions, since he has to apply case decisions handed down over previous years and interpret statutes.

Even if you lose a jury or bench trial, you still have the right of appeal to the Court of Appeals where a panel of judges will decide whether the trial judge was correct in his rulings.

Pleading Guilty with the Right of Appeal

A court may allow you to plead guilty but preserve your right of appeal or you can plead not guilty and ask for a *trial on the record* (TOR). A TOR occurs in just a few minutes' time. You plead not guilty and police reports are read into evidence. The judge then finds you guilty and pronounces sentence. Once you know the sentence,you can better decide if you wish to appeal.

General Denial

"We must indeed all hang together, or most assuredly, we shall all hang separately."
—BENJAMIN FRANKLIN (1706-1790)
at the signing of the Declaration of
Independence, July 1776

"He reminds me of the man who murdered both his parents, and then, when sentence was about to be pronounced, pleaded for mercy on the grounds that he was an orphan."
—PRESIDENT ABRAHAM LINCOLN
(1809-1865)

You have no duty to testify, present evidence, or to give an opening or closing argument. You have the complete right to sit silently in the courtroom during the entire case.

There are cases where the defense lawyer will use the strategy of merely cross-examining state's witnesses, testing their credibility and memory. At the end of the case, your lawyer argues that the prosecution failed to prove the charges beyond a reasonable doubt. I fall twelve jurors unanimously agree, you are free. The prosecutor has a high burden of proof.

The reasonable doubt sufficient to acquit is doubt that would cause a reasonable man to hesitate to act in the more important affairs of his own life. *Beyond a reasonable doubt* does not mean beyond any shadow of a doubt.

The jury may suspect that you are guilty. You may be the most likely suspect. Perhaps you were caught with stolen property nearby and are in a compromising position. You may have made admissions or confessions indicating that you have guilty knowledge of the crime. Notwithstanding, the jury must still be firmly convinced of your guilt. The government must prove each element of the crime offense beyond a reasonable doubt.

Alibi

"Bad alibi like dead fish. Cannot stand the test of time."
—CHARLIE CHAN

"None of us were driving, Officer, we were all in the back seat."

If you were at another place at the exact time the offense was committed, you could not have been the person who committed it. The burden of proof is on the prosecutor to prove your presence at the scene of the crime. You have the burden of proof to come forward to prove that you were somewhere else. If you can satisfy the jury of a reasonable doubt of your presence at the crime scene, you are entitled to an acquittal.

The prosecutor can present rebuttal witnesses, attacking the credibility of your alibi witnesses. You must reveal the names of your witnesses in advance of trial. He will investigate and check out their stories as to how they happened to remember that they (and you) were at another place months earlier.

Eyewitness Testimony

Courts are permitting expert witnesses to debunk eyewitness accounts. Eyewitness cases are some of the most difficult ones to win unless the defense attorney can exploit flaws in eyewitness testimony.

Some attorneys call experts to explain potential flaws of eyewitness testimony, and they're helping clear people accused of everything from robbery to murder.

Considerable psychological research proves that eyewitness testimony is frequently wrong. One law school study shows that eighty-one percent of eyewitness testimony has been proved to be wrong by later DNA testing. Eyewitness testimony plays a major role in convicting more than half of all people sentenced to death.

In many cases, strong witness confidence has little to do with accuracy. Studies show that witnesses often mistakenly identify suspects, especially when police conduct lineups improperly—e.g., showing the same person in multiple lineups or making comments such as "Good choice." Identifications are less reliable when a witness and the suspect differ in race or ethnicity, such as whites identifying blacks or vice versa.

In robbery cases, often suspects are understandably focused on a gun rather than correctly identifying a suspect's face.

When defense attorneys present experts on eyewitness testimony, prosecutors object on the grounds that it "invades the province of the jury."

Of course, lineups should be conducted to eliminate possible bias, and those conducting photo or personal lineups should not be involved in the investigation of the crime. Done incorrectly, sequenial lineups make it easier for police to lead eyewitnesses toward a particular suspect. But for those wrongly accused by eyewitnesses, it can be a matter of life and death.

Eyewitness cases are difficult cases to defend. The trick is to compare the witness's initial statements to the police and their pretrial deposition testimony with their testimony in court. If inconsistencies develop, then the witness may be lying.

> Rule: If the jury believes the witness is lying about small matters, they will not believe the witness on larger important matters.

Circumstantial Evidence

Circumstantial evidence means that direct eyewitness identification or testimony may not be required to convict you. Circumstantial evidence can completely prove the case as long as every circumstance is consistent with the hypothesis of guilt and inconsistent with innocence.

> Rule: Circumstantial evidence cases are legal if all of the facts are consistent with guilt. If a victim swears in court that the crime was committed and points you out as the perpetrator, a submissible case is made against you. Then it is up to the jury.

Motions to Suppress

"There is a way to do it better. Find it."
—THOMAS E. EDISON (1847-1931)

When all looks hopeless, you can file numerous pretrial motions and have evidentiary hearings before your trial actually starts. Sometimes it takes real imagination for your lawyer to come up with constitutional arguments and objections.

Prior to your trial, your lawyer should challenge police questioning of you by asking for a hearing outside the presence of the jury. The purpose is to ask the judge to suppress evidence illegally obtained in violation of the Fourth or Fifth Amendments of the United States Constitution.

If the search exceeded legal limits or if the questioning of you wa illegal, then under the Fruit of the Poisonous Tree Doctrine, the evidence or result of the police work should be excluded from the case.

Motive

"Sometimes nothin' can be a real cool hand."
—PAUL NEWMAN (1925-)
Cool Hand Luke, 1967

"Anybody can kill anybody."
—LYNETTE "SQUEAKY" FROMME (1974)
Would-be assassin of
President Gerald Ford

You may defend on the grounds that you had no reason to do the crime. The existence of criminal intent (known as *scienter*) is essential. It is presumed that you intended the natural and probable consequences of your act, but such intention is difficult to prove directly. The jury must view all the facts to determine whether there is criminal intent or guilty knowledge. It may be proved by indirect evidence and inferences reasonably drawn from circumstances surrounding the incident. The prosecution is given wide latitude to prove motive.

Rule: **Strangely, the prosecutor is not required to prove motive but may let the jury speculate. It then falls upon you to demonstrate lack of any motive or reason to have committed the crime. This may be your best defense.**

Speedy Trial

"It's not that we lost the game. We just ran out of time."
—VINCE LOMBARDI (1913-1970)
Green Bay Packers

Once criminal charges are filed, you have the right to have your case quickly resolved. To assert your Sixth Amendment right to a speedy trial, you must make known your wish by filing a Demand for Speedy Trial.

The U.S. Supreme Court in *Barker v. Wingo* (1972) provided a four-factor balancing test. The conduct of the prosecution is weighed to determine whether you have been denied your constitutional rights. The judge will consider:

1. The length of the delay
2. The reason for the delay
3. Your assertion of your right for a speedy trial
4. Prejudice to your case from the delay

Federal courts attempt to try your case within two months unless you request a delay and sign a Speedy Trial Waiver. State courts are required to try your case in six months from the date your case is filed in circuit court, but there are many exceptions and the law is absolutely of no value. If you claim police delayed their investigation before charges were filed, you ask for dismissal because of preindictment delay.

Rule: **Many cases are delayed for years, but precious few are ever dismissed for failure to receive a speedy trial. First, few defendants ever really want a speedy trial. Delays always work to the advantage of the defendant. Second, the most difficult of the four-part balancing test is showing how your case was prejudiced, e.g., that eyewitnesses to the crime who would have supported your testimony or testified to your innocence have since died or cannot now be located.**

Voluntary Intoxication

"But they also have erred through wine . . . they are swallowed up by wine . . . they err in vision, they stumble in judgment."
—Isaiah 28:7

"Beer is proof that God loves us and wants us to be happy."
—Benjamin Franklin (1706-1790)

If you make the conscious decision to become intoxicated, it is not a defense of a crime. Only if it was involuntarily induced (someone threatened or tricked you into drinking) is it a defense, or if your intoxication is a disease tantamount to a psychosis.

On the other hand, the jury is allowed to consider your degree of intoxication as a factor in affecting your mental state at the time of the crime. Alcohol may diminish your capacity which means that the crime was committed under an altered mental state.

Ignorance of the Law

Ignoratio legis non exusat (ignorance of the law) is no excuse. You cannot plead ignorance, although a jury may consider it in determining your motive or in assessing punishment. Every person is bound to know the law.

Entrapment

The prosecution must prove your predisposition and willingness to commit a crime if the opportunity is presented to you to break the law. Rules against entrapment protect innocent citizens from being drawn into criminal acts by undercover cops or snitches.

To use an entrapment defense, you must admit that you did, in fact, commit the crime, but you allege that the original idea was planted by the police. The mere fact that undercover informants helped provide a favorable opportunity to commit the crime is not entrapment. The jury will decide whether you were predisposed to commit the crime.

Sorrells v. United States (U.S. Supreme Court, 1932) considered the subjective view which focuses on your state of mind and whether you were predisposed to commit the crime. Current Missouri law, based on this case, says that the accused must raise an affirmative defense to prove his state of mind.

A few states use the objective view which concentrates exclusively on the conduct of the police. In this view, your predisposition to commit the crime is irrelevant.

The government may not overstep the line between setting a trap for the unwary innocent and the unwary criminal. They must establish that prior to first being approached by government agents, you were predisposed to commit the crime for which you were arrested.

Insanity

"Support mental health—or I'll kill you."
—BUMPER STICKER

In 1843, Daniel M'Naghten, a Scottish woodcutter, suffered from the delusion that he was persecuted by the Pope and British Prime Minister Robert Peal (who founded the London police force known as the "Bobbies"). He set out to shoot Sir Robert, but by mistake shot Peal's secretary, Edward Drummond. Although there was public outrage, M'Naghten was found not guilty by reason of insanity.

The M'Naghten Rule held that a man is not responsible for his criminal acts if because of disease, his mind does not know the nature and quality of his acts, or does not know that they are wrong.

Missouri has a modified rule. If a suspect is suffering from a mental disease or defect excluding responsibility, he is entitled to have a mental examination prior to trial. If all agree with the mental examination test results, the suspect is committed to the Division of Mental Diseases and is acquitted of the criminal charges. If the attorneys and the judge cannot agree on this procedure, then it becomes a jury question. Intoxication or drug usage are sometimes presented as causes of a type of temporary insanity called "diminished capacity." Under this rule, a person may be found guilty of a lesser crime that carries a lesser punishment.

If you are unable to cooperate with and assist your lawyer in your defense, you are sent to a mental institution until such time as you can later proceed to trial. Thus, there are two stages in which you must be found sane: At the time of trial in order to aid your own defense and at the time of the crime in order to be found guilty.

The war of the psychologist and psychiatrists occurs in trials where both the prosecution and the defense produce expert witnesses. The psychologist does the testifying—psychiatrists do the treating.

Juries weigh expert evidence heavily unless there is conflicting expert evidence. In such an instance, juries tend to totally disregard the conflicting testimony and decide the case as if there were no psychiatric evidence at all.

All persons are presumed sane. You have the burden of proving insanity.

Most crimes require some "state of mind" (*mens rea*), an element of the offense that must be proved beyond a reasonable doubt. The question of mental disease is important in determining whether you did or did not have such a state of mind.

Four mental states required in Missouri are: (1) purposefully, (2) knowingly, (3) recklessly, and (4) criminally negligent. If you are provoked or intoxicated or act in self-defense, you may not have the required mental state. It takes more than just suspicion and a mere emotional disturbance, alcoholism, or drug dependence. Amnesia is not a defense.

Rule: If you intend to claim insanity, you need to be examined by a psychologist or psychiatrist immediately after your arrest. All neighbors and witnesses should be interviewed and all evidence gathered. You will have the burden to convince the jury of your insanity.

Commitment of the Mentally Ill

Laws provide for commitment of the mentally ill. If police arrest a suspect they believe is mentally ill and likely to injure himself or others if allowed to remain free, the officer may petition the court, even without medical certification, to have the person temporarily committed.

With the certification of two doctors, a person may also be involuntarily committed by a friend, relative, spouse, or guardian. The person is entitled to a hearing within five days.

The *Diagnostic Statistical Manual* (DSM) is the bible for doctors to determine what is or is not a mental disease. The human brain is the most complex organ of the body.

If acquitted by a jury or judge on the grounds of insanity; you are confined to the state Division of Mental Health (Fulton State Hospital). The confinement is forever unless and until such time as the director certifies that you can conform your conduct to the requirements of the law. Every six months a patient can petition for a hearing on whether he has been cured to the extent allowed by law.

Thus, on some relatively minor and insignificant crime, it is possible that a person can be confined for life. However, on extremely serious felonies, a person could be confined for only a few months.

There have long been many arguments as to the quality of care given at mental institutions. Absent prolonged and permanent administration of medication and the willingness of the person to voluntarily take medication and submit himself to regular therapy when freed, there is often little else that can be done.

If you suspect a long prison sentence, it is wiser to plead the insanity route, particularly when there is sound medical testimony supporting it. If given a viable choice, juries would much prefer the lesser route, that is, to send you to a hospital rather than send you to prison.

Post-Traumatic Stress Disorder

In the aftermath of the Vietnam War, post-traumatic stress disorder has been discovered. A victim of this syndrome has continued delusions from a period of time when he suffered a trauma or shock due to the deaths of others. He may feel loneliness and despair because he survived and his friends didn't and may commit crimes to draw attention to himself or punish himself for being a survivor.

Withdrawal of Medications

What if you commit a crime after failing to take prescription medication? Upon arrest, you'll be forced to go back onto your regimen. After months of treatment, government doctors then pronounce you fit to stand trial. Indeed, to the jury, you appear quite normal.

One trick is to go off all your meds a month or so before trial. By the time of trial, what doctor can swear you are normal? And besides, shouldn't a jury be allowed to see you the way you were at the time of the crime?

Be aware that the guards may force-feed you medicine (against your will) if court ordered.

Ex Post Facto

No law can be *ex post facto* or retrospective, applying to events occurring before its enactment. Neither can it be used to the disadvantage of a person already accused. The Constitution seeks to give fair warning to citizens and provide advance notice as to whether conduct is against the law.

A law is *ex post facto* if it:

1. Punishes as a crime an act previously committed that was legal when committed.
2. Makes more burdensome the punishment for a crime after its commission.
3. Deprives one charged with a crime of any defense available according to the law at the time the act was committed.

Thus you may not suffer disadvantage from a new law enacted since the commission of the original crime. If it substantially disadvantages you by removing some existing statutory or legal right, its use against you is forbidden.

The Good Faith Defense

This defense is largely used in regulatory and administrative law crimes where you relied on expert advice or made a mistake of law or fact and believed in good faith that you had permission to act. The argument could have some jury appeal.

Double Jeopardy/Collateral Estoppel

The Fifth Amendment prohibits *res judicata,* or double jeopardy. This protects you from:

1. A second prosecution for the same offense after acquittal on the first.
2. A second prosecution after conviction on the first.

3. Multiple punishments for the same offense.
4. Multiple prosecutions for the same offense (splitting or carving out different small crimes).
5. Prosecutions from multiple jurisdictions (municipal court, state court, federal court). This protection was established in *Waller v. Florida,* U.S. Supreme Court, 1970.

If you were previously involved in a civil suit that has some bearing on your criminal case, you may be able to argue *collateral estoppel.* This means that if certain questions were decided in your favor during the civil trial, the prosecutor in your criminal trial cannot raise them against you. It is not *res judicata*, which refers to a prior *criminal* case. You must claim, on some narrow ground, that the prosecution is now being permitted to reprosecute and litigate some fact or theory that failed in a prior civil case. *Collateral estoppel* does not operate as an acquittal so much as to resolve a particular issue that the prosecution seeks to prove.

Statute of Limitations

The law requires that criminal conduct be prosecuted within a specified period of time. If you can prove that your criminal conduct, including the last of the overt acts, occurred three to five years earlier, then the statute of limitations would have expired and criminal prosecution is forbidden.

Unconstitutionality of Law

If you are being prosecuted under a law that is vague, indefinite, or difficult to understand, it should be brought to the judge's attention immediately. If the judge agrees, the law should be declared unconstitutional and the charges dismissed.

Selective Prosecution

**"Your Honor, with your permission,
I'd like to play the race card now."**

If you can prove that police, in the conscious exercise of selectivity of enforcement, deliberately discriminated against you on the grounds of race, religion, or some other arbitrary classification, then your equal protection rights have been violated.

The burden of proof is heavy. You must show 1) that others similarly situated have not been prosecuted but that you were singled out; and (2) that police discriminatorily selected you in bad faith to prevent the exercise of your constitutional rights.

Necessity

If you committed an act to prevent some significant imminent harm and there was no adequate alternative, you can claim your act was done out of necessity. For example, protesters charged with criminal trespass at an abortion facility might claim that their actions were necessary to prevent the killing of unborn children. You must show that you were faced with two evils and chose the lesser one, that you acted to avoid imminent harm and reasonably believed your conduct would abate the greater harm, and that there were no legal alternatives available. More than mere civil disobedience is required.

Travelers Exemption

Persons traveling on highways in a peaceable journey through the state can carry a concealed or otherwise illegal weapon as long as they're on a continuous journey through the state. If they turn aside from the lawful journey to otherwise engage in some unlawful activity, they forfeit the benefit of this exemption.

Police Misconduct

"Major Strasser has been shot. Round up the usual suspects."
—CLAUDE RAINS (1889-1967)
as Captain Louis Renault
Casablanca, 1942

"Decency, security, and liberty alike demand that government officials shall be subjected to the same rules of conduct that are commands to the citizen ... our government is the potent, omnipresent teacher. For good or for ill, it teaches the whole people by its example. Crime is contagious. If the government becomes a law breaker, it breeds contempt for the law; it invites every man to become a law unto himself; it invades anarchy. To declare that in the administration of the criminal law, the end justifies the means—to declare that the government may commit crimes in order to secure the conviction of a private criminal, would bring terrible retribution."
—JUSTICE LOUIS BRANDEIS
(1856-1941)
Olmstead V. U.S.

"The police are not here to create disorder. The policeman is there to preserve disorder."
—CHICAGO MAYOR RICHARD DALEY
(1902-1976)

The judge may dismiss charges if the conduct of police is so outrageous that due process principles absolutely bar a conviction. The difference between passive tolerance of misconduct versus conscious direction by police is sometimes a fine one.

Violations and improper conduct by police that might form the basis of motions to suppress evidence include the following:

- Continued questioning of a suspect after he insists on a lawyer;
- Planting of cellmate informants;

174

- Conducting secret interrogations without an attorney present;
- Psychological coercion to secure confessions;
- Denial of means to contact a lawyer;
- Making promises regarding the outcome of the case;
- Falsely advising a defendant that a co-defendant has confessed;
- Failure to consider the physical condition of the suspect, including the probability of his being on drugs, alcohol, or suffering from a mental disability;
- Conducting lineups without giving the defendant's lawyer an opportunity to be present;
- Conducting physical examinations or special tests without knowledge of the lawyer; and
- Threatening to place your children in a foster home unless you confess.

Sue the Cop

Admit Nothing. Deny Everything. Make counter-accusations.

Like an ordinary citizen, a police officer may be sued for civil damages. Civil liability of a police officer has two separate aspects:

1. Liability for unintentional acts (negligence); and
2. Liability for intentional acts (punitive).

For unintentional acts, a police officer is held to the standard of care of an ordinary and prudent man in similar circumstances. In determining whether an officer's conduct meets the standard of care required of him, he is given the benefit of particular knowledge he has as a police officer which caused him to act in the manner he did.

Many incidents of potential civil liability for negligence arise out of the officer's operation of motor vehicles. Traffic laws of the state exist for the protection of all its citizens. Ordinarily, you may be held liable for negligence if your violation of a traffic law results in injury to an innocent person. Police are given special authority to violate the state traffic statutes. The police may:

1. Park improperly.
2. Run a stoplight or sign, but only after slowing down as may be necessary for safe operation.
3. Exceed the speed limit as long as life and property are not in danger.
4. Disregard traffic signs and signals if emergency equipment is on.

In order for a police car to qualify as an emergency vehicle, the siren or light must be activated and the officer must be on a true emergency mission. Police do not have unlimited authority to ignore traffic control devices. When chasing a fleeing suspect, the officer must weigh the possible advantages to be gained by apprehension of the suspect against the potential danger to innocent citizens.

There are several intentional acts that may result in lawsuits. A common charge is false arrest. This may occur anytime a police officer makes an arrest for a felony when he lacks probable cause.

Malicious prosecution involves bringing a charge when probable cause is lacking and the arrest has malice.

It is common for police to communicate among themselves and use terminology in reference to suspects that would, under other circumstances, be slanderous (spoken) or libelous (written). Usually (on grounds of public policy) these communications are privileged and not within the rules imposing liability for slander or libel.

Police may be sued by the victim of an alleged assault when the victim contends that the officer, without justification, used unnecessary force and violence. An integral part of a police officer's duty is making arrests. Those arrested do not always give the arresting officer their utmost cooperation. Courts permit the officer to use whatever force is reasonably necessary to effect an arrest.

Rule: Everyone wants to sue the police officer, especially after being cleared of charges. Your odds of winning are small, and such suits are generally a waste of time and money. Coordinate your case with your criminal lawyer and a new civil lawyer who brings fresh reason. Let's face it, there is nowhere for you to go to get your good name and reputation returned.

Upon acquittal, most of my clients want to file a lawsuit against somebody. I listen politely, refer them to. a good civil attorney, and rarely hear from them again.

Police may be sued in state or federal court. The most common such action is a federal lawsuit for willful deprivation of federally secured civil rights or the infliction of unnecessary punishments (known as a 1983 *lawsuit*, named after 42 United States Code, Section 1983).

Withdrawing the Guilty Plea

Tendering a plea of guilty to the court is a solemn act that is not to be lightly regarded. There is no absolute right to withdraw a guilty plea either prior to or after sentencing. If you believe an error was made and you have been wronged, the burden is on you to establish grounds that would justify allowing the withdrawal of the plea. The court will look at how much time has elapsed, the prejudice to the prosecutor, and whether your initial plea of guilty was truly understood, voluntary, and freely made.

"The ordinary man is passive. Within a narrow circle (home life, and perhaps the trade unions or local politics), he feels himself master of his fate . . . but (otherwise) he simply lies down and lets things happen to him."
—GEORGE ORWELL (1903-1950)
Inside the Whale

When Can I Be Arrested and Searched?

Warrantless Home Entry

"The poorest man may, in his cottage, bid defiance to all the forces of the Crown. It may be frail, its roof may shake; the wind may blow through it; the storm may enter; the rain may enter; but the King of England may not enter; all his forces dares not cross the threshold of the ruined tenement."
—Sir William Pitt (1708-1778)
before the .British House of Commons

The prosecution has a heavy burden to justify going into a home. Physical entry into a home is the chief evil that the Fourth Amendment prohibits. A firm line is drawn at the threshold of the door. It may not be crossed without a search warrant, and then only carefully and under strict rules.

Police may not enter a home to make a warrantless arrest absent consent or some emergency circumstances, as follows:

1. The gravity or violent nature of the offense;
2. If the suspect is armed;
3. The degree of probable cause;
4. The degree of belief that the suspect is inside;
5. The likelihood of escape if not swiftly apprehended;
6. The peaceful circumstances if not swiftly apprehended; and

7. The peaceful circumstances of the entry.

A warrantless search is legal if:

1. The immediate area is within easy reach or control.
2. A consent to search is obtained.
3. Other possible dangerous persons are present, then other rooms may be searched for weapons. This is called a protective sweep.

Items observed in plain view may be seized, but drawers, closets, suitcases, or closed containers may not be searched without a search warrant or consent. If you're arrested outside your house, you may not be taken inside for the sole purpose of searching.

Stop and Frisk

The U.S. Supreme Court in *Terry v. Ohio* (1969) ruled that circumstances falling short of probable cause for an arrest may justify a *temporary stop and frisk* of a suspect (temporary detention), as long as the cop can prove suspicion of criminal activity. A police officer may briefly detain and interrogate a suspicious person to determine his or her identity and to momentarily maintain the status quo while obtaining information.

If police observe conduct that a reasonably prudent person with police experience would view as suspicious, they may approach a suspect, identify themselves, and ask questions. The necessary reasonable suspicion can be provided by an informant or by the officer's personal knowledge.

Stopping a crime before it happens is just as beneficial to society as apprehending a criminal after the crime has been committed. Consequently, if an officer has reason to suspect that a crime has been, is being, or is about to be committed, then he can make an arrest.

Police cannot detain you to search for mere physical evidence. If the officer has reason to believe you are armed, he may pat you down for his protection or the protection of others. If the frisk results in the finding of a weapon, it is admissible as evidence. If the item does not feel like a weapon, it cannot be removed.

Justification for a frisk includes the following:

- Gait and manner of the suspect;
- Demeanor of the suspect, such as nervousness;
- Officer's knowledge of suspect's background;
- Strange bulges in suspect's clothing;
- Time of night or day;
- Conversations overheard by officers;
- Any suspicious third persons present;
- The street or area of town involved;
- Any known recent criminal conduct in a high-crime area;
- Flight or attempted escape of suspect;
- Minority race in a Caucasian neighborhood; and
- Other unusual observations by the officer.

If you refuse to stop, reasonable force may be used. If you are detained for a long time, it will be treated as an arrest and the court will require the officer to prove full probable cause. You may be asked for an explanation of your actions. Identification will be requested. If your answers are deemed unsatisfactory or contradictory, they may serve as an excuse for your arrest.

If, during a pat-down search, a weapon or evidence of a crime is discovered, you may be arrested. A frisk may not be used as a pretext to search for evidence. There must be reason for the officer to fear for his safety.

Rule: **You may be stopped and frisked even though there is not sufficient probable cause to arrest if you are observed engaging in unusual conduct that reasonably leads a cop to believe that criminal activity is occurring and that you· are armed and dangerous; the officer identifies himself and makes reasonable limited inquiries as to your conduct; your response and actions do not relieve the suspicions and fear of danger to the officer. If you are approached by police and do not wish to be questioned, ignore the officer and walk on. Make him stop you. Courts may treat it as an arrest, and if it is without probable cause, it can be suppressed.**

When Can I Be Placed in a Lineup?

A lineup is a legally arranged confrontation between an accused and the victim.

The U.S. Supreme Court in *United States v. Wade* and *Gilbert v. California* (1967) held that any lineup conducted after the filing of formal charges is a critical stage in the criminal proceeding, requiring the presence of a lawyer. If a witness has identified the accused at an illegal lineup, the witness cannot testify to the lineup or identify the accused in court until a separate hearing is held. This hearing must establish by clear and convincing evidence that the in-court identification had an independent source, is based upon observations of the suspect at the scene of the crime, and is free of any primary taint from the illegal lineup.

Some states require a lawyer even at the preindictment lineups. Missouri requires counsel only after the filing of formal charges.

If a defense attorney appears, he should be present only as a mere observer. Prosecutors should not participate either. The names of all people present are noted, and those people may later be subpoenaed as state witnesses. If the suspect has a lawyer appear, the state will have an easier burden of proof to show the lineup was fair.

Five or six persons of approximately the same age, weight, height, complexion, race, and manner of dress as the accused are carefully selected. Once the lineup is assembled, a photograph is taken of each lineup participant and the witness is allowed a separate view. The exact words of the witness are noted, and nothing is suggested to the witness encouraging identification.

It is permissible to have lineup participants move in any direction, walk, move arms or legs, remove glasses, shave, reveal tattoos, put on different costumes, wear a hat, or speak nontestimonial statements such as "This is a stickup," "Give me your money," or "I'll blow your head off." The accused's voice may be an identifiable physical characteristic.

A lineup card is given to the witness who then circles the proper number corresponding to the person identified. The card is dated, signed by the witness, and retained by the police.

A bad lineup does not automatically stop an in-court identification, but there is a heavy burden on the state to prove that the witness' in-court identification was not affected by the lineup. Witnesses are under obligation to swear that their in-court identification is based solely on observation of the suspect at the time of the crime.

An accused has no right to refuse to submit to a lineup. Reasonable force may be used to compel participation. If the accused absolutely refuses to stand or participate in a lineup, his refusal can be commented upon at trial.

Emergency Identification

If there is an imperative need, a suspect may be returned to the scene of a crime for immediate identification.

The *Wade-Gilbert* rule of right of counsel does not apply to an on-the-scene confrontation between the suspect and the witness. However, the following guidelines *do* apply:

1. *Mental state of the witness.* Police should avoid giving the witness the idea that they have captured the suspect. Police should tell the witness, "We have a person who may know something about this case or who may be a witness in this case," without saying anything further. The witness should volunteer his identification.
2. *Avoid custodial appearances.* Once the suspect is brought before the witness, he should not appear in handcuffs or surrounded by officers.
3. *Avoid delay.* On-the-spot confrontations must be conducted within minutes after the crime, near the crime scene. If a long delay occurs, the officer should conduct a regular lineup. Emergency identifications are sometimes necessitated by the severity of the victim's injuries.

Mug Shot Lineups

When a suspect is not in custody but his mug shot is available, it is possible to conduct a mug shot lineup by placing before a witness the suspect's picture along with other filler pictures.

Exact identification of the facial features should first be obtained from the witness so comparable mug shots can be secured that demonstrate those particular features. The mug shots should be marked in order, placed in an envelope, and preserved as evidence.

The witness is shown an array of photographs (not just a single photograph of the accused). At trial, the photos should not be referred to as "mug shots" or show the prison numbers.

Lineup Guidelines

In order to successfully combat defense charges of a suggestive lineup, police do the following:

- Obtain a signed Waiver of Counsel and Consent to have the lineup;
- Record the name of the suspect's attorney if he is present;
- Record the name, age, date of birth, height, weight, and position of each person who participates in the lineup;
- Record the names of all police officers present;
- Record the date, time, and location of the lineup;
- Write brief notes about what happened during the lineup;
- Arrange for the lineup participants, insofar as possible, to be the same general age and race, have similar physical characteristics, and wear similar clothing;
- Take a color photograph of the lineup;
- Require all lineup participants to perform physical movements or verbal statements uniformly;
- Do not have the suspect appear in handcuffs or indicate his identity to the witness in any manner;
- Do not permit more than one witness at a time in the lineup room;
- Do not allow witnesses to talk with each other;
- Do not permit witnesses to view photographs of the suspect prior to lineup identification;
- Do not draw any special attention to the suspect;
- Do not engage in unnecessary conversation with witnesses or permit unneeded persons in the lineup room;
- Record comments made by witnesses; and

- Furnish each witness with a lineup identification form.

Lineup Warnings

Prior to a lineup, warnings must be given to the suspect:

1. Although you do not have a right to refuse to appear in a lineup, you do have the right to have a lawyer present.
2. If you are unable to pay for a lawyer, one should be appointed to represent you during the lineup free of any cost to you. Good luck!
3. Where voice identification is desired, the police officer should say, "You and the other participants in the lineup will be asked to repeat certain words, phrases, or sentences spoken by the person who committed the crime."

Rule: **Missouri guards against the *substantial likelihood of irreparable misidentification* and uses a three-part test to decide whether a prior improper lineup should void the in-court identification: (1) the presence of an independent basis for identification; (2) the absence of any suggestive influence by others; (3) positive courtroom identification.**

The purpose of a lineup is not only to identify the guilty, but to clear the innocent.

Rule: **If you are requested to stand in a lineup, you have no choice. Assert your rights to speak with an attorney immediately upon arrest.**

Your Fourth Amendment Rights

The Fourth Amendment protects your reasonable expectation of privacy from unreasonable invasions by the police.

"We are not dealing with formalities. The presence of a search

184

warrant serves a high function. Absent some grave emergency, the Fourth Amendment has interposed a magistrate between the citizen and the police. This was not done to shield criminals nor to make the home a safe haven for illegal activities. It was done so that an objective mind might weigh the need to invade that privacy in order to enforce the law. The right of privacy was deemed too precious to entrust to the discretion of those whose job is the detection of a crime and the arrest of criminals."
—*CHIMEL V. CALIFORNIA* (1969)
U.S. Supreme Court

If the evidence is obtained in violation of the Fourth Amendment, it will be held inadmissible and excluded from trial.

With the possible exception of cases where private property must be entered to make an arrest, there is no constitutional requirement that an arrest warrant be obtained. A warrantless arrest occurs where it is reasonable under circumstance, and the arresting officer has probable cause to believe the accused is committing or has committed a crime.

How Far Can They Search?

"For good or ill, our government teaches the whole people by its example."
—FORMER JUSTICE LOUIS BRANDEIS (1856-1941)
U.S. Supreme Court

The first ten constitutional amendments adopted by the new republic are the Bill of Rights, intended to be a limitation on the government. It is a shame today that most Americans don't even know what these rights are.

Police have no right to make an arrest on a whim and no right to make an unreasonable search and seizure of citizens and their property. If a search is planned by police, a search warrant must be issued by a judge. Most searches are not planned and therefore warrantless. To be legal, they must fall within specified categories of areas where there are exceptions to the warrant requirement.

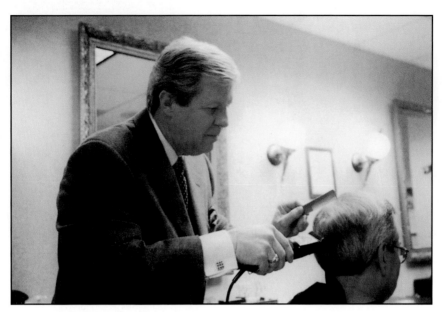

The lawyer's job is to carefully examine every hair of evidence . . .

Examine every item of the state's evidence and get your own trail exhibits ready.

To blend the ingredients of law to the facts . . .

to carefully avoid any missteps . . .

It is important to select a good jury of independent thinkers . . .

Researching the law . . .

. . . to the highest authority . . .

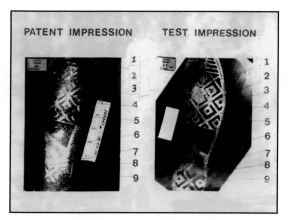

Evidence of shoes . . .

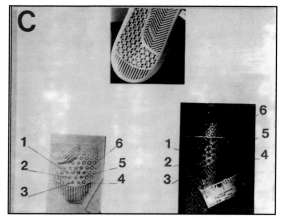

heals . . .

must match up . . .

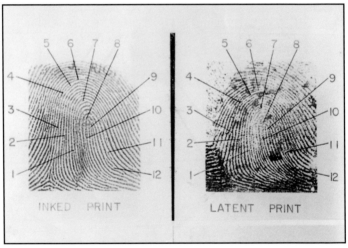

like the hoops and swirls of a fingerprint.

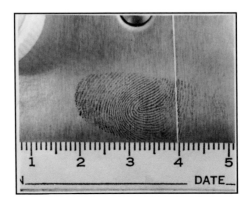

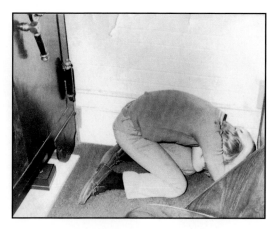

Police take photos at crime scenes . . .

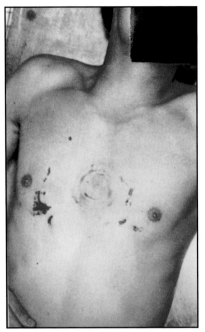 

to solve the crime . . .

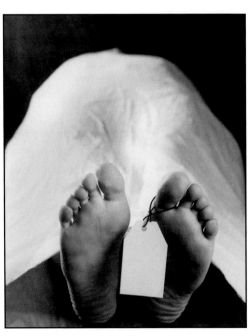

. . . in the end.

What is a search? A search takes place whenever a citizen's privacy is invaded in the course of a criminal investigation, and things are taken by police in the course of looking into books, papers, and items in a person's home or business.

What is an unreasonable search? Your right to be protected from an unreasonable search is open to various interpretations depending upon the facts of each case.

When can there be a search without warrant? There need not be a warrant provided the search is for things otherwise seen in plain view, you consent to the search, there are emergency circumstances, or the search is incident to a lawful arrest.

If police are in hot pursuit, or are conducting an inventory search in order to check contents of your vehicle to prevent loss at a later time, or if you are engaged in suspicious activity, you may be legally stopped and frisked.

Persons, Papers, Effects Generally Not Protected

The protection of the Fourth Amendment is not required for the following:

- Any object within plain view
- Open fields
- Grounds around a house (curtilage)
- Objects accidentally discovered at a car accident
- Items voluntarily shown to police
- Items found during a lawful inventory
- Conversations overheard without electronic aids
- Items recovered from dead persons
- Public places
- Looking through open windows and doors
- Vacated premises
- Jails and prisons
- Common areas accessible to the public
- Telephone, utility, or bank records
- Abandoned articles

Reasonableness of Search

The Constitution protects you only from unreasonable searches and seizures. There are no clear means of ascertaining whether a search is reasonable but criteria include the following:

- Was a warrant obtained?
- Was there time to obtain a warrant?
- Was the search conducted during the day or at night?
- What was the place subjected to the search?
- What was the scope of the search?
- Was force or coercion employed?
- What was the purpose of the search?
- What was the crime under investigation?

The Constitution does not define unreasonable searches. The judge will rule on a case-by-case basis.

Objects of Search

The scope of search is justified by the circumstances that rendered it permissible.

When police are searching under the authority of a warrant, the objects of the search must be specified. With or without a warrant, any search must be reasonably limited and justified by the initial reason. Thus, in a homicide investigation in which the search is for a weapon, police are not justified to go through someone's personal papers.

Legitimate objects of a search include weapons, evidence of crime, fruits of crime, instrumentalities of crime, or contraband.

Items coming within plain view during a lawful search may be legally seized even if not listed on a search warrant.

Incident to a Lawful Arrest

The exception to the requirement of a search warrant is whether or not the search is incidental to a lawful arrest. To determine this:

- There must be an actual arrest.
- The arrest must precede the search.
- The arrest must be lawful.
- The arrest must be in good faith and not just an excuse to search.
- The search must be for articles connected with the arrest.
- The search must be close to the arrest in time and place.
- The search must be reasonable.

When there is probable cause to arrest, there is always the right to search the person to protect the officer and ensure his safety. The same is true to protect your property during the booking process.

The U.S. Supreme Court (*Chimel v. California,* 1969) limits searches to areas into which a person might reach to destroy evidence or weapons. The *constructive reach or lunge doctrine* allows a search into areas where you might jump or grab a weapon or evidence, such as a desk, glove compartment, dresser, or closet.

It is a common police tactic to ask for identification and then search either the drawer or wallet where you reach. It is a common ruse to encourage you to walk into various rooms to get clothing, make telephone calls, or use the bathroom. Then, police can conduct a search of all these areas within the home. Look out!

Rule: **Do not allow police inside your home unless they have a search warrant. Do not open the door! If police have an arrest warrant, get your personal belongings together and quickly exit your house, slamming the door behind you. Once they are in the home, they will refuse to leave and you will never get them out. The sanctity of the home was the main concern of the Bill of Rights.**

A common problem is the search of briefcases, handbags, or suitcases carried by or located near an arrested person. The search of items carried by a suspect or located near him is allowed.

Some courts do not allow the search of luggage and other similar items in circumstances where they could be easily secured and a search warrant later obtained. Searches are more easily allowed when an officer testifies that he feared for his safety.

The Schmerber Doctrine

In *Schmerber v. California* (1964), the U.S. Supreme Court considered a DWI suspect who was forced to submit to the withdrawal of a small blood sample for analysis. The court upheld the search provided it was limited and done in accordance with medically accepted standards with due regard for health. The search did not violate the right of the suspect against self-incrimination since it took physical evidence, not words.

As long as the physical intrusion is not a substantial one, does not endanger life or limb, or is not enough to shock the conscience or be offensive to one's sense of justice, the following intrusions have been held to be legal:

- Fingernail scrapings.
- Giving voice or handwriting samples.
- Swabbing the hand and performing a paraffin test.
- Palm prints and fingerprints.
- Use of fluorescent lights.
- Courts allow surgical bullet removal if there is no other way to obtain the evidence. A presurgery hearing is held and a qualified surgeon performs the operation.
- Use of a solution compelling you to vomit.
- Use of reasonable blood tests.
- Requiring a urine sample.
- Waiting a reasonable time for a bowel movement.

Body Searches

For police to make embarrassing body searches (anal or vaginal), the following rules must be followed:

1. There must be a clear indication that the intrusion will supply important evidence.
2. It must be accomplished by a safe, reliable method, no more psychologically uncomfortable than reasonably necessary.
3. The court will weigh the probable worth of the evidence against

any alternative means for obtaining evidence.

Strip searches are allowed of prisoners in jails where they no longer have constitutional rights to be let alone or have any expectation of privacy.

The Booking Search

Once you are arrested and taken into police custody, your clothing and property may be taken, searched, and inventoried for safekeeping. This is a part of the routine booking process. Should the arrest later be held to be illegal (not based on probable cause), then the booking search is likewise illegal.

While under arrest, you may be made to:

- Be photographed
- Be videotaped
- Be fingerprinted
- Speak
- Allow blood to be medically withdrawn
- Participate in a lineup
- Put on specific clothing
- Take a benzedrine test for recent weapons firing
- Exhibit your body or display scars or birthmarks
- Undress and have clothing inspected and seized
- Have hair samples plucked
- Place your hands under ultraviolet light
- Shave or alter your appearance
- Give saliva or urine specimens
- Take a Breathalyzer test

Once admitted to jail, you retain little expectation of privacy. Anything you do or say that is observed by a jailer or other prisoners is legally admissible in court. If you are booked in jail, ask to telephone a good friend or attorney. While on the telephone with an attorney or friend, direct them to ask you questions so that you need only reply "yes" or "no." Anything else overheard by jailers can be used against you at trial. Otherwise, keep your mouth shut!

Trash

Police may search through trash left at the front curb or back alley of a house. The U.S. Supreme Court (*California v. Greenwood,* 1988) ruled that a homeowner does not have a reasonable expectation of privacy in trash left outside of the home.

Garbage and trash left for collection are immune from any claim of privacy under the Fourth Amendment. Trash is readily accessible to animals, children, scavengers, snoops, or other members of the public.

It appears that a person must live the life of a mole in order to claim constitutional Fourth Amendment protection. When you place trash in a tied trash bag and place it inside a trash receptacle or container then leave it near a curb or sidewalk (still on your own private property), you have no constitutional rights of privacy. Make sure you do not discard anything illegal!

Abandoned Property

If you discard items someplace outside your house or its immediate area (known as the curtilage), even though it is beyond your physical control, police may seize such property on the grounds that it is abandoned. They are not required to prove that you intended to abandon the property permanently.

If the property is discarded within your house, hotel room, vehicle, or another place under your control, it is not considered abandoned.

Rule: **The test as to whether there has been abandonment is whether you still have a reasonable expectation of privacy that society is prepared to recognize.**

Aerial Searches

Plane or helicopter overflights of residential areas at a relatively low height in order to view, inspect, and photograph are illegal but nonetheless allowed. Only if it can be said that you erected high fences, roofs, or canopies, or demonstrated your expectation of privacy, would the evidence be disallowed.

> Rule: **Even if the overflights are in clear violation of FAA rules, police spotter planes can photograph your fenced backyard.**

Plain Smell Doctrine

The scent or odor of illegal drugs smelled by police familiar with the odor, or by trained marijuana-sniffing dogs, will support probable cause for a further search.

Investigatory Searches

There are limited times when police can forcibly interfere with a person's liberty on less than probable cause:

1. A reasonable search for weapons for his protection (stop and frisk);
2. A border patrol checkpoint stop; and
3. Routine detention of residents in a house while it is being searched under a search warrant.

In these situations, courts engage in a balancing test to see whether the detention and search are lawful. They must weigh the following factors:

1. The public concerns served by the seizure;
2. The degree to which the seizure advances the public interest; and
3. The severity of the interference with individual liberty.

Emergency Searches

Police may conduct searches in emergency (exigent) situations where life or limb may be in danger.

Originally, exigency cases related only to where there was threat or danger to life. If police believe life is endangered, breaking into a home by force is not illegal if reasonable under the circumstances.

The law now allows emergency searches in situations where police have reasonable grounds to believe that evidence might be destroyed. This is just another lost constitutional safeguard. Examples include the following:

- A trash fire where items were being destroyed;
- Where there is a threat of destruction of drugs;
- The sound of flushing toilets or running water; or
- The sound of running feet.

Courts insist upon a good-faith belief that a real emergency did exist. Circumstances vary and the court will carefully consider the following:

- The degree of urgency involved and the amount of time necessary to obtain a warrant;
- Reasonable belief the contraband is about to be destroyed;
- The possibility of danger to police guarding the site while a search warrant is being obtained;
- Information indicating that the suspect was aware that police were on his trail; and
- The ready destructibility of contraband and the knowledge that efforts to dispose of narcotics and to escape are characteristic behaviors of those engaged in narcotics trafficking.

Impounding Premises

The U.S. Supreme Court carved out a small exception in a few specifically established and well-delineated situations in which cops can search a house without a search warrant. A strong burden rests upon police to show the existence of an exceptional situation, excusing the necessity for a search warrant under the *Chimel* doctrine.

When an arrest occurs inside a house, police will guard the door to prevent the destruction of evidence while obtaining a search warrant. They have limited power to exclude you from your home.

Inspection Searches

In certain limited administrative situations, city, county, or state laws require the inspection of certain licensees who engage in a government-related business or a business that requires a government permit or license (i.e., firearm dealers, restaurants, packing plants, bars, liquor stores).

Such searches are usually conducted by surprise, but administrative officials conducting the search should:

- Announce their purpose
- Search at reasonable hours (although not necessarily convenient to the licensee)
- Search without force (unless a formal search warrant may also be obtained)
- Act on their own and without police collusion

If you refuse inspection, the inspector must obtain a search warrant, but your refusal could be the basis for revocation of the license or for other sanctions provided by law.

Administration inspection searches have been allowed in fire prevention, food inspection, trash collection, agricultural, and gun license inspections where the need for surprise is recognized as apparent. Inspection searches are official conduct authorized by law. Whatever minor invasion of privacy may occur is outweighed by the need of the inspection system and the overriding public interest in the inspection as a credible deterrent to crimes or hazards.

Airport Pat-Downs

You have few constitutional rights as an air traveler but you can request a private screening with a same-sex screener. Unfortunately, some airports do not have curtained-off areas or same-sex screeners.

- *Wanding* means outlining the body front, back, and between the legs. Wands work without contact.
- *Quick whisking* requires an occasional touch without any rubbing or poking.
- *Pat-downs,* touching breasts or near the genitals is called for only if a screener can't resolve a beeping metal detector.
- *Backhanding* is used by experienced screeners, which is a pat-down with the back of the hands which seems to be less upsetting to passengers who are less likely to interpret it as groping.

Tips on how to sail through the airport screeners include:

- Remove every bit of metal possible before going through the security checkpoint. Underwire bras, shoes, or boots with steel reinforcements or taps on heels will set off the detector.
- If you have surgically implanted metal, speak up so that the searcher can work more efficiently. Travel with a card or note from your doctor verifying the implant.
- Before you leave home, purge your hand luggage of items no longer allowed on flights after September 11, 2001. Manicure scissors, cork screws, and pocketknives should be left at home. Butane lighters and long tweezers may be confiscated.
- Don't carry wrapped packages. They'll likely be opened at security.
- During a pat-down, be calm and respectful. Know that you have the right to ask that it be done by a person of the same sex and in a private area.
- Keep your arms up and forget about being modest.
- If you have a complaint about the manner in which a search was conducted, contact the security checkpoint supervisor. If you feel the search was highly professional, you should say, "Thank you," words rarely heard by screeners.

Search of Students

Street crime now spills over into the classroom. Murder, possession of narcotics, stolen property, or guns, assault, robbery, and rape are occurring more often on school property.

Searches conducted on university campuses and dormitories are judged by different standards than those in secondary schools. Minors are subject to a greater degree of supervision. Yet neither teachers nor students completely shed their constitutional rights at the schoolhouse door.

A student does not enjoy much of a reasonable expectation of privacy in his locker and personal property. The Fourth Amendment applies only to police searches and is aimed at controlling arbitrary illegal conduct of government agents. If the school search is conducted by school officials acting in concert with police, the search is legal but is governed by the higher Fourth Amendment standards.

If the search is by school officials only, the U.S. Supreme Court in *New Jersey v. TLO* (1985) applies a two-part test: (1) Was the search legal at the start? (2) Was the search reasonable?

The Doctrine of Loco Parentis

Loco parentis is an ancient law that places the government in the role of a lawful parent. A teacher is given parental authority to carry out her duties. Courts invoke this doctrine to justify the reasonableness of searches. School officials must have latitude in controlling the school environment and balancing the personal privacy of the student against the need to maintain order in schools.

School officials possess duplicate keys or combinations for lockers. Teachers are empowered to consent to a search by police officers.

School Safety

Inside school, some students are made to wear bar-coded photo ID badges. Some classrooms have "black boxes" with mirrored eyes staring implacably down from the walls.

Schools have responded to campus shootings by clamping down

on all sorts of security problems, from fights to theft, vandalism, graffiti, and intruders. Students have signed waivers agreeing to random searches, and to waive any expectation of privacy when tightened security is in effect.

As a result, some schools now have:

- Perimeter fences to delineate school property and secure cars after hours.
- Microdots—tiny microfilm hidden inside expensive equipment so that it can be identified if stolen.
- Black box cameras—video camera systems throughout the school to monitor classrooms when requested by the teacher.
- Screamer boxes—transparent shields installed over the fire alarm to film who actually pulls the alarm.
- Swipe tests—a school official wipes a student's hand with a special paper (swipe), which is then sprayed with a substance. If it turns purple, it shows there is evidence of the specific drug being tested for.
- Exterior cameras—high-resolution color cameras monitor the grounds to reduce vandalism and theft.
- Cameras on school buses—cameras in black box enclosures when requested by the driver.
- Badges—everyone on campus receives a badge and lanyard to identify him or her as a school member.
- Metal detectors—all people entering the school are scanned with handheld detectors to locate metal.
- Security personnel—a sworn officer, usually with gun and patrol car, or a security aide with a radio.
- Hand geometry reader—measures the height and width of fingers and compares the information to an internal database. The device can be used in elementary and preschools to identify adults picking up students during the school day.

Parents Can Be Sued

It's not about anger or revenge. It's not even about punishment. But crime victims injured by a teenager sometimes want to sue the teenager's parents. It's a wake-up call just to send a message.

Parents can be taken to task for the sins of their children under an emerging set of laws and court rulings known as "parental-responsibility laws." Sometimes teenagers will commit trivial mishaps, school pranks, vandalism, or malicious mischief. Some laws make it a felony for parents to recklessly allow their children to use guns or commit crimes.

The Missouri law is a slap on the wrist, allowing a crime victim to sue for up to $1,000.

Some civil cases use the theory of vicarious liability; which stipulates that parents must pay for damages caused by their child if a parent should have known of the damage a child was about to inflict, and the child acted carelessly; recklessly; or negligently.

Homeowners insurance may cover some of the damages if the complainant can show negligence of the parents.

Criminal charges against parents are hard to prove. A parent may be found guilty of endangering the welfare of a minor, especially if they knew the child was planning to commit a crime and/or had prior knowledge of the child's actions. Usually parents cannot be prosecuted on criminal charges unless state law specifically punishes a parental lapse.

Search by Private Citizens

The protection of the Fourth Amendment does not apply to private persons not acting pursuant to a request by police or acting under color of law.

Even though there may be an otherwise illegal restraining of a suspect or a completely illegal search where entry is made without the consent or knowledge of the occupant, the evidence can be handed over to police and used in court.

The exclusionary rule of the Fourth Amendment is applicable only to prevent government misconduct.

Rule: **The Fourth Amendment does not limit citizens from aiding in the apprehension of criminals. It only restrains police.**

The only remedy a citizen has is the right of a civil lawsuit against those who wrongfully took such property. Nonetheless, the evidence seized remains admissible in both state and federal courts.

Items searched for or seized by the following persons may be admissible into evidence:

- Foreign border officials
- Foreign officials
- Private investigators
- Insurance agents
- Airline employees
- Husbands or wives
- Private persons
- Garage or service station personnel
- Motel or hotel owners or housekeeping personnel
- School teachers
- Utility meter readers
- Cable television installers

Search of Mail

When you're in jail, your mail is opened. Jailers intercept and read all mail unless it is marked *attorney-client*. You have no expectation of privacy.

The Inevitable Discovery Doctrine

The U.S. Supreme Court in *Nix v. Williams* (1984) (known as the Christian Burial Speech case) said that if the evidence ultimately and inevitably would have been discovered by lawful means (even if initially discovered illegally), it is admissible at trial. Having juries receive probative evidence is in the public interest and is properly balanced by putting the police in the same, not a worse, position than they would have been had not police error or misconduct occurred.

Police were looking for a small girl's body and obtained information as to her whereabouts illegally, in clear violation of a *Miranda* warning given to the suspect. The suspect had an attorney and asserted his right not to talk. The two officers talked to each other, lamenting that if they knew the girl's whereabouts her parents could give her a Christian burial. With this indirect questioning, the accused spoke up and confessed. Since volunteer searchers were combing the shoulders of the highways, the court decided that the girl's body would have been ultimately discovered by legal means, and allowed the evidence and conviction of the defendant although his confession was disallowed.

> Rule: **If the police commit an illegal search but are able to convince the judge that the evidence would have been inevitably discovered through lawful means, it will be admitted in court.**

Search Warrants

A search warrant application must:

- Be in writing
- State the time and date of the application and the crime
- Name the place to be searched and the things sought
- State the date of the facts relied on
- Show probable cause
- Be verified and filed in court
- Be signed by the judge
- Command all things seized be accounted for within ten days

Warrants that fail to specify the person, place, and thing to be searched are known as *general warrants* and are forbidden.

A search warrant may be issued for:

1. Stolen or embezzled property
2. Any weapon, tool, or thing used as a means for committing a felony
3. Property for which possession is an offense
4. Property used by owner as a raw material in manufacturing

anything for which possession is an offense
5. A kidnapped person, deceased fetus, or corpse
6. Obscene matter
7. Any person or movable thing
8. Papers or private records
9. Evidence of any crime

Preparation of Search Warrant Application

Every police agency has search warrant forms from which they can quickly prepare warrants.

They have a set policy with the prosecutor as to whether he is to assist in preparing the application before it is given to a judge. Police should prepare the search warrant and two copies for the judge to sign.

The following rules apply:

- A warrant cannot be overbroad. An exact description and itemization of all articles and things sought should be listed on the warrant application and not be left to the officer's discretion. A negligent misrepresentation by an officer does not void the warrant, but an intentional one does. The description must identify the property with sufficient clarity that the officer executing the warrant can reasonably find it.
- A description or diagram of the place to be searched should be given as accurately as possible, sufficiently described so that the judge can say the police knew with sufficient particularity the area to be searched. Description by street and number is sufficient; it is not legally necessary to name the owner.
- All reasons for wanting the warrant must be listed in detail:

    1. *Personal observation.* If the officer has personally seen the crimes, he should state how and on what date he happened to see them, attach copies of his reports to the search warrant affidavit, and include any personal

expertie he may have.

2. *Hearsay.* A warrant may be justified by hearsay information (even if double hearsay), but it must include from whom the information was received. Probable cause may be based upon information received through an informant and corroborated by other proof within the officer's knowledge. Information from fellow officers is automatically considered reliable, as is information from ordinary citizens.

3. *Reliable confidential informant.* An informant is not reliable simply because he has supplied information in the past; his information must be corroborated. His track record of reliable information must be stated. If possible, he should be made to sign an affidavit. Whenever possible by surveillance or investigation, police should verify an informant's information, which adds to the reliability and may give probable cause where the tip was given by an anonymous informant. If the informant was a witness to the crime rather than a participant, his presence may be demanded at trial to show he is not guilty, or to disprove entrapment. If reliability can be shown, his name need not be given. If reliability cannot be shown, other corroboration is sufficient, such as from another informant, or any sufficient detail to show that it is more than a casual rumor or that it is an admission against interest.

- It is vital that police include all of the underlying circumstances in the application and attach the written affidavits of other officers. An application for a warrant is good or bad on its face (known as the *Four Comers Rule*). Even if the affidavit contains some unlawfully obtained information, but the untainted information establishes probable cause, it is legal (known as *dissipating the taint*).
- Once police take the application to a judge, the judge holds a nonadversary hearing to see whether sufficient facts have been stated. Missouri does not permit the officer to supplement the written papers with oral testimony. A later reviewing court will

WHEN CAN I BE ARRESTED AND SEARCHED?

only consider the written affidavit.

Misstatements in the Affidavit

In *Delaware v. Franks,* the U.s. Supreme Court allows an individual to challenge the truthfulness of the affidavit (known as a *Franks* hearing). There must be proof of deliberate falsehood or reckless disregard for the truth. It must be more than mere inaccurate information. There must be evidence that it was intended to deceive or mislead the judge.

Who Signs the Search Warrant

Any judge can issue a search warrant. Time is of the essence, and often judges are contacted on off-duty hours when they are away from the court. The officers must wait for the judge's clerk to type and prepare the actual warrant, which the judge signs. The judge must personally sign the warrant and cannot delegate the authority, although a judge from another jurisdiction may act.

A warrant application must be sworn to and signed before the judge. It must state the time and date. The warrant must be executed with reasonable promptness, since it expires in ten days. A late return does not void the warrant unless it was intentional and deliberate.

Police may stay on the premises only during the time reasonably necessary to search and seize the described property. The search should be as brief as reasonably possible. Prosecutors should never participate in the service of a warrant, but they often do.

Search of Persons on Premises

Searches of persons on the property can be justified if:

- The search warrant identifies those persons;
- The persons consent;
- Police reasonably believe that the individuals are armed or dangerous; or
- There are factual grounds for custodial arrest and incidental

215

search.

The U.S. Supreme Court in *Ybarra v. Illinois* (1979) ruled that the mere presence of a person at a search warrant scene does not give police the right to search him.

Upon completing the search, an officer should be assigned at the scene to make at least two copies of an inventory, listing in detail each item seized. Inventory sheets are taken to the scene and copies of the warrant and inventory are left in plain view with the person in charge. All items seized must remain in the custody of the officer who signs the inventory until further written court order. Unfortunately, it doesn't always happen. Watch the chain of custody of seized evidence as it is sometimes loose.

The prosecuting attorney should not accompany a sheriff in serving a warrant in the absence of exceptional circumstance, since he might become a trial witness and could not then also act as prosecutor.

Serving the Warrant

Police should act in a reasonable manner. They should knock and announce their identity and purpose. Unannounced entry is permitted only in emergency situations where a person is in peril of bodily harm or evidence is being destroyed. All necessary force can be used to enter the place to be searched. Once entry is gained, the warrant should be read in its entirety to the person in charge. Other officers may be asked to assist as deemed necessary and may enter by other doors or windows. They cannot, however, enter the premises before the officer serving the warrant. The search need not be made in the accused's presence or in the presence of any occupant. Police can enter an empty home.

A search warrant should be served during the daytime (if there is enough light to recognize a man's features at ten yards). If the search begins in the daytime, it may extend into the night provided that officers executing the warrant act reasonably and do not delay.

A nighttime warrant may be obtained but will be granted only if the affidavit states that the affiant is positive contraband is in the place to be searched. The search warrant may state that the search can take place at any time.

Taking Items Not Named in the Warrant

If evidence of a different unsuspected crime is discovered, it may be seized under the *plain view doctrine,* but newly discovered evidence must be readily identifiable as contraband. There must be a *nexus* between the items seized and the criminal behavior. Some prosecutors prefer "piggyback" search warrants, leaving one officer in charge of the premises while other officers return to prepare an additional search warrant for newly discovered items.

Reasons that might justify some delay in searching are as follows:

1. Waiting for occupants to return to develop a possessory offense.
2. Waiting for the occupant to leave if officers believe he might destroy evidence.
3. More officers are needed to search the premises and time is needed to group them.
4. Bad weather conditions.

Good Faith of Police Officer

Even evidence discovered in the course of serving an illegal search warrant will not be excluded, irrespective of the actual validity of the warrant, if the officer acted in good faith and acted in objective reasonable reliance on the warrant. This is known as the Leon Good Faith Doctrine, and remains it politically controversial.

Rule: Smart cops may claim typographical errors and insist they were acting in the best faith possible. Search warrants are difficult to suppress.

When Can They Search My Car?

CHAPTER 9

"Under the automobile exception to the Fourth Amendment requirement of a search warrant, police may conduct a warrantless search of a car as thoroughly as a judge could authorize it if an application was made for a search warrant."

—U.S. v. Ross
U.S. Supreme Court (1982)

This chapter is easy. When can cops search your car? The answer is, darn near any time they want to, and there is precious little you can do about it.

FBI statistics show that seventy-five percent of all crimes include the use of an automobile, and courts relegate vehicles to a special class by themselves. Search warrant requirements have been eased since vehicles can be driven easily to another jurisdiction where police have no authority.

A lesser degree of reasonable grounds is necessary to search an automobile than is required to search a home.

Courts go further in upholding a search if it was a protective search (i.e., the officer felt his life might be in danger). Where the officer can testify to facts showing that he was in possible fear of his safety, courts are inclined to give him necessary safety and protection. (Thirty percent of all shootings occur when an officer approaches a person seated in a car during a traffic stop.)

A search for physical evidence can follow a simple traffic stop only if there is reasonable belief that the car's contents offend against the law. A driver's person can always be searched when arrested. A search of the entire car on a purely exploratory fishing venture is not allowed unless the driver reaches into the interior of the car where a weapon could be obtained.

Automobile stops may be made for:

- Giving a summons or making a traffic arrest
- Routine traffic investigation
- Probable cause to believe a crime has been committed
- Investigative detention (stop and frisk)
- Probable cause to believe the vehicle is stolen
- Roadblocks, if searching for a particularly described vehicle
- Checking serial number, engine number, drivers license, or plates
- Seizing contraband in the vehicle
- Safety inspection stops
- Narcotics interdiction checkpoints
- Border searches

Police can stop an automobile to make a routine check for an operator's license. You and your passenger may be made to exit the car. It is not a crime to fail to produce a driver's license, but failure is presumptive evidence that you are unlicensed. Once stopped, if police develop a cause to search for evidence, the interior of the car may be searched, including the trunk, locked glove compartment, or under the back seat.

> Rule: **The vehicle should be searched in the immediate vicinity of the arrest. Even if you are handcuffed, guarded, or lying on the ground, your vehicle can still be searched.**

Your car can be towed to police headquarters and searched immediately for evidence or weapons if the officer has a good reason for removing the car to headquarters rather than searching at the scene. Possible reasons include the following:

- The search might create a traffic hazard or congestion
- An unruly crowd has gathered and the officer fears a riot
- It is too dark to see properly
- The automobile itself is being seized as an item of physical evidence in the case

> Rule: **The search must be contemporaneous with the arrest. If the time lapse is a significant one, a search warrant should be obtained and the vehicle kept under surveillance to avoid the later contention of evidence planting. The time lag should not be an unreasonable one under the circumstances.**

> Rule: **The arrest must be lawful, must be based on probable cause, and will be measured by the facts known at the time of the arrest. It cannot be a convenient excuse, subterfuge, or pretext for conducting a search.**

Courts allow cops to search the following areas:

1. Under and behind the front seat
2. Backseat
3. Glove compartment
4. Trunk
5. Closed containers in the car

Rule: **The automobile is not a magic world in whose presence the Fourth Amendment completely disappears, but it might as well be. Evidence taken during car searches is difficult to suppress.**

Vehicles Other Than Autos

Mobile homes and camper trailers are treated like all vehicles unless located in a trailer park, in which case a search warrant must be obtained.

Truck trailers, when connected to a cab or parked, and U-Haul trailers are treated the same as automobile trunks. If the trailer is parked without a cab overnight or longer, a search warrant is needed.

Public passenger vehicles, buses, planes, trains, and boats may be halted to arrest a suspect and a limited search performed of the area under his control.

Privately owned boats and planes may be searched without a warrant and are treated like mobile homes.

Stop and Frisk of Automobiles

Courts allow police the right to stop a motor vehicle on suspicion not amounting to probable cause. Using the same line of reasoning in *Terry v. Ohio* (a stop and frisk on a sidewalk), an officer can stop a car or reach into a stopped car if he believes criminal activity may be occurring (*Adams v. Williams*, 1970). The officer must identify himself, initiate limited questioning, require you to identify yourself, and make reasonable inquiries concerning your activity. In the course of a temporary investigative detention, when contraband is seen in plain view or other evidence of a crime discovered, it is admissible at trial.

Police are not permitted to stop every car that passes. They must:

- Believe a crime may have been committed
- Have reasonable grounds for such belief
- Show absolute necessity for immediate investigatory activity

Such situations include the following:

- An officer observes an item within a car that is believed to be stolen
- Car left hurriedly from a store believed to have been burglarized
- Car matches description of an auto observed earlier at burglary
- Officer is instructed by radio to arrest for stealing
- Driver's evasive action (furtive movements)
- Existence of suspicious facts leading officer to believe the trunk contains contraband
- Suspicious collection of clothing, burglary tools, stolen revolver, or items believed stolen
- Emergency circumstances

Inventory Search

The U.S. Supreme Court in *South Dakota v. Opperman* (1986) allows police to take custody of an unattended vehicle. To keep the vehicle and its contents safe, they may search the vehicle or locked containers to protect the contents. The officer's motive must be protective and not investigative, and not a pretext merely to search for evidence of a crime.

Standard police procedures regarding inventory searches must be in writing (a department regulation), but courts rarely enforce this law.

Rule: **To successfully attack an inventory search, you must prove there was a reasonable alternative to impoundment, or another responsible person to drive the car home, or that police don't always impound and search cars in similar circumstances.**

An abandoned car can be seized and searched without a warrant and without probable cause. Rights to possession are relinquished at the time of abandonment. Stolen vehicles may be searched without a warrant. A car thief has no right to object to a search.

Impoundment of a vehicle is unnecessary:

1. Where other passengers could have taken charge of the auto
2. If a friend could have removed the car within a few hours
3. If the suspect would be absent only for a brief time to post bond
4. If police could have driven the car to a nearby parking area where it would be reasonably safe
5. If police don't usually compound and search
6. If police have no written standard policy

Search of Closed Containers Found in Car

The search of closed or locked containers is allowed under the moving vehicle exception to the Fourth Amendment's warrant requirement.

A closed box, luggage, sack, knapsack, or other container may be opened and searched without a search warrant so long as the police have probable cause to believe something illegal is within the container.

Search and Destroy

For the past decade, the u.s. Supreme Court has been hammering down the coffin lid containing the remains of your right of privacy in your car. The Fourth Amendment is explicit about your freedom from unreasonable searches, guaranteeing your right to be left alone. However, when you are in your car—forget it!

There are a number of exceptions to the Fourth Amendment developed in court rulings over the past two hundred years. Police do not need a warrant to conduct a search if:

1. They are in hot pursuit of a fleeing suspect
2. They have strong reason to believe a serious crime is about to be committed
3. They see contraband in plain view
4. You consent to a search
5. They search within your grabbing distance in the process of an arrest

There is a double standard with regard to your car. Police are not permitted to search your home without first getting a warrant—but take your suitcase from your home and put it in the trunk for a drive to the airport and suddenly you have little expectation of privacy. The potential for police abuse is clear.

Drinking and Driving

Nothing I say should be construed as a guarantee of freedom from arrest or an endorsement to drink and drive. But if you've made the wrong decision and decided to drink and drive, what is the best way to avoid a serious accident? If you're behind the wheel, have had a couple of drinks, and feel a buzz, do this:

1. Roll down a window, turn off the heater and stay awake.
2. Drive in as straight a line as you possibly can. Keep your vehicle entirely within your own lane.
3. Don't drive slower or faster than the posted speed limit.
4. Concentrate on stop signs and red lights since your reactions are slower than you think.
5. Don't listen to soft music as it will lull you to sleep.
6. Be more cautious than usual.
7. If you feel drowsy, stop, get coffee, and stretch your legs. Pull over to a safe place off the road and sleep for a while. Getting home late is better than not getting home at all.
8. If there is any question as to whether you should drive, exercise these options: walk to a bus stop and ride; walk home; call a friend or relative; call a taxi; walk to a motel and take a room. Try anything, but don't make a live bomb out of your car.

Drunk drivers are taking our lives and the lives of our loved ones:

- Approximately two thousand people a day are injured and seventeen thousand people a year are killed as a result of drunk driving—one person every thirty minutes.
- Fifty percent of all Americans will be involved in an alcohol-related accident sometime during their lifetime.
- Forty percent of all fatal accidents involve alcohol.

Rule: **Despite all punishments handed out by judges, our nation's families and societies in general continue to suffer the effects of drunk driving. The sobering truth is that deaths and injuries caused by drunk driving are not accidents—they are the tragic result of reckless choices.**

When the Siren Comes On

Suppose you are being pulled over and you've been drinking. Popping breath mints, dousing your mouth with pocket breath spray, or smoking cigarettes only tips the cop you have something to hide. Don't be stupid enough to be caught with an open container that can be seen anywhere inside your car.

You will be asked to exit your vehicle and walk to a safe location. The officer will want to give you a balance test, finger-to-nose test, gaze nystagmus test (following your eyes), and an ABC test. During these tests he will be filling out an *Alcoholic Influence Report Form* that grades you on how you react, as well as your breath, actions, eyes, clothing, and attitude.

Rule: **Be as cool and calm as you can. Don't joke around and attempt to be funny or you'll be considered drunk. Wait for the officer to tell you step by step what to do. Don't volunteer conversation. Following his instructions is part of the test.**

Quick Test Before Driving

If after a few drinks you want to test your own abilities prior to getting behind the wheel:

1. Recite the alphabet quickly, smoothly, and without hesitation.
2. Walk a straight line for ten steps, heel against toe. Turn briskly and repeat in the opposite direction. You can't stagger, pace your steps, or stumble without turning.
3. With head level, eyes open and ahead, raise your left foot six inches off the floor and hold it there for ten seconds. Now do the right foot.
4. Stand at attention, arms down, head tilted back, eyes closed. You should be able to stand still without swaying back and forth.

What Will Get You Arrested

Just because you've been drinking doesn't mean you'll automatically go to jail—it's your ability to operate a vehicle that is important. The cop's decision will be based on:

1. Your driving, breath odor, speech, eyes, and balance.
2. Your attitude—is it belligerent? Overcooperative? Combative? Is there a sudden change in attitude from one extreme to the other?
3. Your physical appearance. Is your hair unkempt? Is food spilled on your clothing? Are you wearing shoes? Is your fly open?
4. The officer's personal expertise in detecting subtle characteristics of a person who has been drinking.

Rule: **The traffic officer is merely enforcing laws that citizens have demanded. We all want to reach our destinations with a minimum of delays or injuries in an overcrowded world. A cop is just another citizen you are paying to protect you from the irresponsible and malicious acts of others. Traffic laws are for your own good.**

In representing DWI clients, I make no apologies for trying to even up the odds to give my client a fair shake and the chance of a fair trial. By the time clients come to meet with me, they have sobered up; they're scared and in crisis. It's a perfect opportunity for me to help them help themselves.

If You Have a Car Accident

No one expects to be in a crash, but these steps could prepare you should one happen:

1. Keep a first aid kit in your car and know first aid.
2. Carry warning devices: a flashlight, flares, or fluorescent plastic triangles.
3. Keep pencil, paper, and identification handy, including your insurance ID card.
4. Survey the scene before you take action. Check for oncoming cars or spilled gasoline, and determine your safety.
5. Check for injuries. Get to a phone, call 911, or ask another motorist to do it. Most people have mobile telephones.
6. Record all police officers' names and badge numbers. Request a copy of the police report and get a file number so that you get a copy later.
7. If your car is creating a hazard or blocking traffic, move your car if possible. If a passenger is injured, put out warning devices and turn on your emergency flashers.
8. Jot down details concerning weather, visibility, road conditions, and how the accident happened. Make a sketch.
9. Admit nothing. Comments such as, "It was all my fault," or "Don't worry, I'm fine," can come back to haunt you in insurance claims or later in court.
10. Call your insurance agent or attorney immediately. All questions should be handled only by them. Refer all phone calls and don't answer questions yourself.

What Are Your Rights?

What should you do if stopped by the police when keeping company with contraband? Even though the cops can search pretty much at will, you can improve your odds:

1. Make sure nothing illegal is in plain view where it could lead to a full search.
2. Police always prefer to search under the consent exception, which allows them to scratch the itch without an arrest procedure if you consent and waive your Fourth Amendment rights. Most people are so terrified when stopped with contraband that they'll go along to appear innocent. When asked, "Do you mind opening your trunk?" respond, "Officer, is that really necessary?" Be respectful. Don't assist in your own bust.
3. If you are pulled over for an arrestable offense, the officer has the right to search the interior of your car. He may choose not to do so. However, be gracious in accepting whatever citation he wants to give you. It may lessen the likelihood of a search. Don't argue.
4. If contraband is found, shut up. Don't add to your own problems. Ask for an attorney. You still have a chance to be acquitted. Your silence cannot be used against you.

Rule: **You have little right of privacy in your car. Sitting in your car gives you about the same claim to privacy as sitting on a bench in a public park. If you transport contraband, what can you do to avoid open season on auto searches? You'd better walk!**

When Stopped, Do Not Exit Car

Even though you may be stopped for a minor traffic violation, you should not exit from your car. The officer may still conduct a search of you and your car (since it is within your immediate area and control) and remove any weapons or contraband. The search may extend to containers, open or closed, found within the passenger compartment.

This includes the glove box.

Don't jump out and approach the patrol car. Stay seated with your driver's license and both hands in plain view.

Commercial Vehicles

Vehicles involved in a regulated industry such as commercial trucking is that the government has a substantial interest in warrantless inspections necessary to further their regulatory agenda. *(New York v. Berger, 1987)*. Thus we have check points and weigh stations.

Law officers have the right to "determine compliance" with commercial vehicle laws, rules and regulations in compliance with *RSMo. 304.230.4*, so expect to be stopped on a whim.

When Can I Be Questioned?

CHAPTER 10

"Many links frequently compose the chain of testimony which is
necessary to convict any individual of a crime . . . that no witness is compelled to furnish anyone of them against himself.
And the court ought never to compel a witness to give an answer
which discloses a fact that would form a necessary and essential
part of a crime which is punishable by the laws."
—CHIEF JUSTICE JOHN MARSHALL
(1755-1835)
U.S. Supreme Court

In *Miranda v. Arizona* (1966), the u.s. Supreme Court required that
all suspects in custody being interrogated by police be advised of
specific constitutional rights. Incriminating statements cannot be
used against you unless you have been advised of your rights.

The courts will consider:

1. *Arrest.* Contrary to popular belief, *Miranda* warnings are not
   technically required after an arrest and do not affect the arrest.
   They are required only when you are arrested and only if you
   are questioned.
2. *No arrest.* If you are not under arrest, the place of questioning
   is an important factor in determining whether custody has at-

tached, requiring *Miranda* warnings.

3. *Police stations.* Questioning at a police station is often held to be custodial even if the questions weren't intended to yield damaging information (or if the person came voluntarily to the station and police knew him to be lying).

4. *Police cars.* If questioning is undertaken in a police car to obtain incriminating statements, warnings should be given and waivers obtained.

5. *Street encounters.* A street encounter is custodial where you are stopped at gunpoint, handcuffed, or questioned about a specific crime. Otherwise, no warnings are required. A policeman may approach you on the street, in a store, or on a bus, train, or plane and question you. A street encounter does not require *Miranda* warnings.

6. *Crime scenes. Miranda* was not intended to hamper police in investigating crime and general on-the-scene questioning.

7. *Homes.* Lateness of the hour, number of officers, directness of questions, and whether officers were invited or not may be factors of custodial interrogation, even when you are in your own home.

8. *Places of employment.* If the crime occurred at the place of employment, it is a crime scene interview. If police are investigating a crime that occurred somewhere else, but there is still a coercive atmosphere during questioning, it is recommended that police give warnings to all employees suspected of criminal activity when there is more than routine questioning.

9. *Search warrant locations.* The legality of a search warrant is not dependent upon *Miranda* warnings. If police have arrest warrants or intend to arrest, *Miranda* is not required. If incriminating evidence is discovered, *Miranda* warnings should then be given.

10. *At the time of transport.* If you are transported to headquarters, you are in custody. It is not uncommon for transporting officers to find a talkative accused. No warnings are required if they are just listening to you blab.

11. *Jailhouse questioning.* Prisoners questioned about other crimes should be readvised of their rights.

Custodial Interrogation

When police are merely investigating, such as in a typical auto accident (where an officer arrives on the scene and questions bystanders), *Miranda* does not apply. If statements are volunteered, they are admissible if you are not in custody. If you are the prime suspect, *Miranda* warnings should precede further questioning. Courts look at the facts known to the officer to determine his intent, as well as whether you might reasonably think you are in custody.

If you claim your rights, any action by police intended to elicit comments is illegal.

Miranda warnings must be given when:

1. You are in custody;
2. You are deprived of your freedom in a significant way;
3. You are under formal arrest;
4. The officer is unwilling to let you go;
5. The officer believes you have committed a crime; and
6. The officer's actions lead you to believe you are not free to go.

If, however, you volunteer information before interrogation begins and before an opportunity to advise you of your rights, any statements may be used against you at trial.

Police carry a *Miranda* warning card. The *Miranda* card is admissible into evidence and is shown to the jury. Many police fail to read both sides of the card (the reverse side recites your waiver of rights).

Waiver of Rights

I have read the warning statement advising me of my legal and constitutional rights and I understand what my rights are. I have been given the opportunity to use the telephone to call an attorney or a member of my own family. I am willing to answer questions and make a statement. I do this voluntarily and of my own free will. I understand and know what I am doing. I do not want to call or consult with a lawyer, and I do not want a lawyer to be present to advise me of my rights and with whom I can consult. No promise of immunity or other promises of any kind have been made to me, and no physical force or pressure of any kind has been used against me to cause me to make a statement. I waive my rights and agree to talk.

Standing alone, reciting the *Miranda* warnings does not constitute compliance with *Miranda v. Arizona* unless you voluntarily and intentionally waive your Fifth Amendment rights.

The following rules should be kept in mind:

1. An oral waiver is good if you make an oral confession. If the confession is written, a written waiver should be obtained.
2. Continuing questioning after you request a lawyer or express a desire to remain silent is prohibited. You cannot be persuaded to waive your constitutional rights. Police must scrupulously honor your request.
3. Silence can never be used as an admission of guilt.
4. The warnings should be renewed every time you are questioned or after delays. Police must stop whenever you wish to stop.
5. If you refuse to talk and later change your mind and wish to make a statement, police must confirm your willingness to talk.
6. If you have a lawyer, you may still waive your rights. Police must obtain a clear waiver from you.
7. If you express the desire to talk with some person other than a lawyer (friend, relative, or employer), you have not asserted your *Miranda* rights. Forget talking to Mama.
8. If you answer some but not all questions, police need not cease their interrogation.

Great care should be taken if you have low intelligence or limited education, are a juvenile, have some physical pain, or are wounded, and courts will consider these factors. If you have been held incommunicado, physically abused, promised leniency, given false promises, or are emotionally upset or threatened, the confession is illegal. The fact that you may be intoxicated or under the influence of drugs may be considered in deciding whether the statement was voluntarily made, but it does not void the confession if you understood what you were saying.

Rule: **It is a common joke that in a DWI arrest, cops will always testify you were intoxicated. Regardless, they will always swear you were sober enough to understand and waive your constitutional rights. Amazing!**

Legality of Confessions

Deception, artifice, and trickery are perfectly legal! The judge will look to see whether the deception was of such a nature as to prompt untrue statements. Then he will decide whether your statements were still reliable.

Once you request a lawyer, all questioning must cease and neither the prosecutor nor the police can comment on your silence, although the prosecutor can argue to the jury your failure to present evidence (but not your failure to testify).

Many cops will run you down or discourage you from talking to an attorney. Don't be intimidated.

You can request a hearing to determine whether your confession is legal. The judge will decide whether your statements are admissible to the jury. You will probably lose. Judges rarely suppress confessions. The jury gives weight and credibility to your statement. They evaluate the circumstances in which it was given and usually side with the cop.

Videotapes or secret recordings of confessions are permissible. There is no requirement that you be told statements are being recorded.

When statements are spontaneously uttered, occasioned by excitement surrounding a crime or auto accident, they are part of the *res gestae* (the excited utterance rule).

Small mistakes given in the *Miranda* warnings are allowed if they are harmless. If the mistakes give rise to confusion, the confession should be suppressed. You will rarely win.

Exculpatory statements are statements made by you that tend to show innocence. *Inculpatory* statements are those that tend to incriminate or show guilt. Unbelievably, the law allows the prosecutor to use incriminating evidence against you at trial but not helpful evidence. This is proof that the similarity between justice and courts is purely coincidental. Your damaging words are admissible at trial but helpful words are not.

Courts look for any clear proof of your desire to waive your rights—showing a knowing intent that could be combined with words, acts, and all the evidence of the surrounding facts and circumstances. It is not required that you expressly state a waiver of your rights.

Officers Posing as Cellmates

It is legal for a police informant to pose as a jail inmate and engage in conversation to obtain the confession of an arrested person. Even though it involves a gross deception, such interrogation techniques have been allowed.

Some suspects engage in jailhouse bravado and want to talk once arrested. Informants are in a unique position of exploiting this vulnerability because the prisoner is under the complete control of the jail.

If arrested and placed in jail, keep your mouth shut and don't discuss the circumstances of your arrest with fellow inmates, many of whom are anxious to become jailhouse snitches.

Traffic Offenses

Miranda warnings do not have to be given to a motorist who is stopped for a minor traffic offense. The following situations do not require a warning:

- To examine your driver's license and registration if stopped for speeding
- To detain you while police check out the possibility of a stolen car
- To ask why plates are expired

235

- When a passenger in a motor vehicle is stopped for a traffic offense and is not subjected to custodial interrogation
- When you volunteer statements after a routine traffic stop
- After stopping a vehicle for driving without lights at night and officers ask a general question about the contents of the vehicle
- When police ask if you have been drinking, ask general questions pertaining to destination and permission to drive a vehicle, or request that you show your license and registration
- When you volunteer information while an officer is writing out a speeding ticket

No Need for Miranda

You always have the choice of waiving your constitutional rights. If you're approached by police at your home or business, or on a street corner and their questioning is noncustodial (you are not under arrest), any statement you make is a voluntary statement. If it is incriminating, it can be used against you and the officer will testify against you in court. Please, walk away. Tell them to leave. Stand up for your right of privacy—to be left alone.

If words are spoken by third persons that normally call for a response, such as your wife making a heated remark during an assault, police officers can testify to what was said and your lack of response (the tacit admission rule).

If you have claimed your Miranda warning rights, you still can be questioned on unrelated crimes. It's tough to know just what your rights are. It takes a Philadelphia lawyer to keep it straight.

Defenses to Keep Out Your Incriminating Statements

Your right to remain silent must be scrupulously honored by the police. Some cops will negligently or intentionally violate your constitutional rights by continuing to pester you with further questioning.

You can file a pretrial motion to suppress (a Jackson-Denno hearing) and ask the judge to exclude your statement on the following grounds:

1. That you were not properly read all of your Miranda rights
2. That you did not waive those constitutional rights and voluntarily speak with police
3. Due to alcohol, drugs, fatigue, medication, physical injury, or limited intelligence, you did not fully understand your constitutional rights
4. That police used duress, threats, and coercion to overcome your will and forced you to talk

Tricks in Obtaining Legal Confessions

"I wish I had an answer to that because I'm tired of answering that stupid question."
—YOGI BERRA (1925-)
New York Yankees

A normal confession is obtained by police advising you of your *Miranda* warning rights, obtaining a written or oral waiver of those rights, and then tape-recording or writing down your exact words.

Contrary to popular belief, confessions may be legally used even if they were obtained through the use of deception and misrepresentation. Confessions obtained through lies or subterfuge are admissible unless the deception is such as to offend societal notions of fairness or is likely to procure an untrustworthy confession. How much deception is enough to meet that requirement?

Police may badger you after you claim your *Miranda* warning rights. Some cops like to talk down, derogate, confuse, or discourage you from talking to an attorney. Defense attorneys are not popular among police. In fact, we're not popular anywhere unless you need us.

Trickery does not render a voluntary confession inadmissible unless it's proven to overbear your right of free and rational choice. Don't worry; you'll seldom win this pretrial motion.

Use of Silence as Evidence

The law is supposed to be well established; an accused's silence at the time of arrest, and especially after receiving his *Miranda* warnings, is not admissible. Postarrest silence should not be mentioned or considered by the jury as any evidence of guilt. To do so would be an impermissible comment on your Fifth Amendment right to remain silent.

However, once you are advised of your Miranda warning rights and waive your right to remain silent, then any speech at all (including silence) may be admitted into evidence and commented upon before the jury.

If you are questioned under circumstances that would call for an answer such as an admission or denial, and where a jury could conclude that only a guilty person would have remained silent, this is admissible:

1. Where you initially refuse to make a statement and later speak in a voluntary manner.
2. Where you claim your right to silence but then continue speaking.
3. Where you incorporate an incriminating statement with periods of silence.
4. Where you refuse to answer only certain questions or inquiries during a general interrogation.

Rule: **It is absolutely best to say nothing. Claim your constitutional rights; do not sign anything. Wait until you've had advice from an attorney even if the police try to talk you out of it using subtle interrogation techniques and threats.**

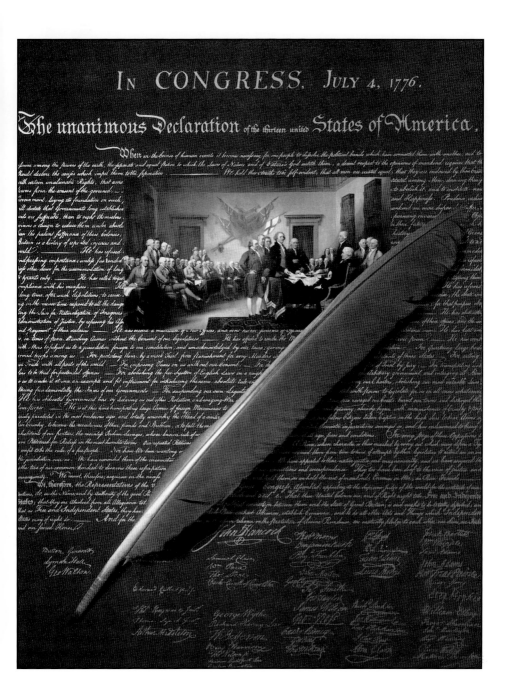

The War on Drugs

"Consider somebody who wants to smoke a joint of marijuana.
If he's caught, he goes to jail. Now is that moral? I think it's
absolutely disgraceful for our government to be destroying their
lives, putting them in jail. That's the issue to me."
—MILTON FRIEDMAN
Nobel Prize-winning
economist, 1991

Since 1985, the nation's jail and prison population has grown one
hundred thirty percent, and has passed two million even as crime
rates sometimes decline.

Behind the increase is a national get-tough mood that has produced longer sentences for all criminals and the end of parole in many
states. Most Americans favor lengthy terms for violent criminals.

Perhaps the biggest single factor is the systematic jailing of drug
offenders. Drug imprisonments have grown more than four hundred
percent in the last ten years, nearly twice the growth rate for violent
criminals. More people are behind bars for drug offenses in the United States (about 400,000) than are in prison for all crimes in England,
France, Germany, and Japan combined.

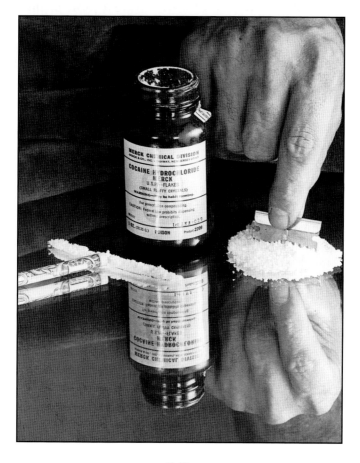

"Up with hope, down with dope."
—MARION BARRY
Campaign slogan of former
Washington, D.C. mayor (after
a cocaine conviction)

Strategies for Defending a Drug Case

There are five basic types of drug offenses: possession, sale to a government agent or informant, possession with intent to distribute, trafficking, and conspiracy.

Possession cases frequently involve narcotics concealed or contained in a vehicle or space not readily associated with the accused. A common defense is lack of personal knowledge of the presence of the drugs. This is called the *mere presence defense,* since the drugs' mere presence is insufficient for the government to convict. There must be evidence of your activity or involvement sufficient to support an inference of constructive possession.

On a direct sale of drugs to an undercover agent, a typical defense is *entrapment.* This defense alleges that you were talked into committing the crime by an overzealous informant. In *possession with intent to distribute,* you can defend on the grounds of possession for mere personal use, or impeachment of the government informant who received a reduced charge or other favorable treatment in exchange for his testimony.

In *trafficking* (the carrying and transportation of drugs), the defense may be lack of knowledge of the drugs if they were in a container, box, or suitcase. This is no good if your personal belongings were intermixed with the drugs or your fingerprints were on the drug package.

In a *conspiracy* prosecution (an agreement to commit a crime), you may have to counter audio/videotapes and transcripts of conversations and cross-examination of informants and co-conspirators who have been given special treatment to testify against you. These are tough cases to beat. Your co-conspirators will roll on you and you become the fall guy.

Proving a Drug Case

It is illegal to possess any quantity, however small, of a controlled drug (unless it's a trace amount). Certain drugs may not be possessed under any circumstance. Marijuana, cocaine, LSD, crack, meth, stimulants, and others may be possessed in limited quantities pursuant to a valid prescription.

It is illegal to manufacture, possess, have under your control, sell, give, distribute, cultivate, grow, or by any process, produce or prepare any illegal drugs.

You may not transport, carry, or convey in any vehicle, boat, or aircraft any illegal drug. A vehicle used to transport any of the drugs is subject to forfeiture by public or private auction with proceeds going to the state. The arresting officer takes possession of the vehicle and secures it in a safe place, then through the prosecutor files a forfeiture petition in Circuit Court declaring the vehicle a public nuisance.

All crimes, particularly drug offenses, must be committed intentionally and willfully, and must be proved beyond a reasonable doubt. The prosecutor must prove that you had the intent to possess, which can be shown by a large quantity of drugs. If only a few particles of marijuana are found in your car, it will be difficult to show that you knew about and intended to possess the drug. Knowledge may be shown by circumstantial evidence or by incriminating statements. Your mere presence in a house along with others is insufficient to establish possession of a drug, but your proximity to the drugs may support constructive possession. The possession of narcotics need not be exclusive where it is reasonable to infer intentional control and possession, but if there is joint control, there must be some other evidence to link you with the drugs. Control of premises is not automatically deemed possession of all things therein. A drug is possessed where the evidence shows you had knowledge of or access to the drug and were involved in its use, which is the concept of constructive possession.

If you are charged with possession of a controlled drug that may be obtained by prescription, you have the burden to prove that your possession is legal.

Prescription drugs legally obtained must be kept in their original container. Stop and read that again. Don't take pills out of their original containers! Pharmacists, physicians, veterinarians, and dentists must keep strict records which are open for police inspection.

It is illegal to possess narcotics paraphernalia or devices for the use of any prohibited drug. You may not attempt to obtain any narcotic drug by fraud, deceit, misrepresentation, subterfuge, forgery, alteration of a prescription or written order, concealment of a material fact, or using a false name or address.

Before drug charges are filed, the drug is analyzed by a qualified chemist. The exact type of drug is determined and the botanical name given (example: marijuana is botanically known as *cannabis sativa*) in order to properly allege the crime. A field test is not legally sufficient.

The most common problems experienced in the prosecution of drug offenses are those of arrest, search, and seizure. The arrest must be legal and there must be probable cause to search. Police try to obtain consent searches whenever possible to avoid these problems.

If the prosecutor has demonstrated a valid arrest, search, and seizure at the suppression hearing and has a valid chain of custody on the drugs, there is little benefit in requesting a jury trial.

In sale cases, the usual defense is entrapment unless you deny the sale. Entrapment means the criminal intent did not originate with your mind but was planted or was the result of the officer's creative ability. If police or an informant solicit, encourage, or induce you to engage in conduct in which you were not ready and willing to engage, it is entrapment.

Dodging a Drug Test

Chances are that if you have applied for a job recently, you have had to submit to a drug est. Today drug testing has increased to nearly ninety percent. Fifty-four cent of the companies that test for drugs are under government mandate to do so. Many members of Congress want to test federal employees' hair, saliva, or sweat for illegal drugs and change standards on heroin testing lowering the level of opiates a person must have in his body to be identified as a potential heroin abuser.

A drug test is really just a marijuana test, since marijuana is the most widely used illicit drug and the one that interferes least with job performance compared to alcohol and other drugs that have painful withdrawal symptoms. Marijuana is virtually the only drug that is not water soluble, with the result that its metabolites—not the drug itself—stay in the system far longer than traces of other drugs. A person who used marijuana two weeks ago is more likely to have his urine test positive than one who used cocaine two days ago.

Furthermore, government testing programs are in an utterly indefensible position because the government allows importation and distribution of hemp products that cause a positive urinalysis. These products include hempseed oil nutritional supplements, candy, cookies, cheese, bread, cooking oil, and general seasoning. These items can be purchased at supermarkets, in health food stores, or by mail order.

There are a growing number of products designed to help your future employees beat a drug test. It is not illegal to make, sell, or use products that falsify drug tests.

Sweat Patch

The latest fad to detect illegal drugs is PharmChek, a skin patch acting as a collector of components of sweat. A two-by-three-inch bandage of adhesive plastic film holds an absorbent pad and is placed against the skin. Manufactured by 3M, it allows oxygen, carbon dioxide, and water vapor to pass so the skin underneath can breathe normally. Larger drug molecules are trapped in the absorbent pad portion of the patch.

People produce three hundred to seven hundred milliliters of sweat each day. The pad catches part of this sweat. The patch can be worn on the upper, outer arm or on the lower midriff, and should be worn for a minimum of twenty-four hours to ensure that an adequate amount of sweat is collected. It is tamper resistant. The advantages over urine testing are as follows:

1. In urine testing, the window of detection of drug use is twelve to seventy-two hours after last use of the drug. The patch catches drug usage for up to seven days.

2. The sweat patch is able to detect four times more cocaine users than intensive urine testing during the same period.
3. Parent drugs as well as drug metabolites can typically be detected and identified in sweat. This is particularly important in the determination of heroin use.

The sweat patch isn't new. Drugs have been detected in sweat since the early 1970s. The method uses the same well-established analysis procedures as urine testing. It is better than hair testing which still not been cleared by the FDA.

The most common ways to try to beat the sweat patch are as follows:

1. Removal of the patch some time after application and reattaching it using Band-Aids or other adhesives
2. Peeling back the upper portion of the sweat patch, removing the absorption pad, and replacing the pad prior to reporting back for sweat patch removal.

Unfortunately, these methods result in an absorption pad that is wrinkled, folded, creased, or otherwise deformed and, therefore, easily detectable.

Drug Testing in the Workplace (Urine and You're Out)

The U.S. Supreme Court has ruled that employer urine testing is legal and regulates a perceived threat to the public and employee safety in the work place. Courts considered whether testing impermissibly infringes upon your constitutional rights.

State and federal governments require workers in certain industries to submit to searches and tests. You do not have to submit to a drug urine test unless it is specifically provided for in your employment contract.

How to Survive a Drug Test

Recreational dopers have been using trusty standbys like soap, salt, bleach, and plain tap water to beat urine tests ever since the government gave employers permission to use them on employees and job applicants fifteen years ago.

Dump a tablespoon of salt or a thimble full of liquid soap or bleach in the sample cup, or fill it a quarter full of tap water before the urinalysis, and there is no way it should read positive. Rules include the following:

1. *Never stipulate.* Never tell anyone you've done drugs. It is amazing how easy it is to get people to admit to pot smoking. Don't admit to anything. Never confess.
2. *Never give morning urine.* Drug metabolites collect and concentrate in the bladder overnight. Make sure your bladder's been emptied at least two times before giving a specimen.
3. *Drink water.* Drug tests count the ratio of drug particles in urine to nondrug particles. Raise the ratio of nondrug particles by drinking water before the test.
4. *Do not despair.* Many private employers do not conform to federal drug testing guidelines. Never abandon your rights. Once they're gone, they're gone forever.

Try to call in sick on test day to delay one more day if possible. It will help.

If you're a user, there are many factors that determine the degree of the test, including metabolism, tolerance, frequency of intake, fluid intake, amount of marijuana, potency of the drug, and the length of time you've been a user.

The famous question, "How long will it take?" is the single most frequently asked question. Don't post or e-mail such a question.

Don't Get Clipped

A relatively new weapon in the war on drugs is scissors. Employers are snipping locks of hair from job applicants and employees. Lab analysis of hair aims to show whether the person has used marijuana, cocaine, methamphetamine, or other illegal drugs within the previous ninety days.

Hundreds of employers turn to hair testing to supplement or replace urine testing. They say drug users have learned to beat urinalysis by adulterating their urine or by abstaining from drugs for a few days.

The fact is if you don't want your hair drug tested when you make application, all you have to do is say "No," and get a job elsewhere.

There is the possibility of hair color bias. Someone with dark hair might be more likely to be caught by the test than a person with light hair. A black person with light gray hair may be less susceptible to being caught than a white person with dark, coarse hair. In addition, marijuana smoke, cocaine dust, and other residue can get into the hair at parties, bars, and other public places.

Hair testing is a reasonably accurate technique, but of course, like urinalysis, it is not one hundred percent reliable.

Field Tests

At the crime scene, police use a quick, presumptive test that utilizes chemicals which have been placed in a special kit to decide whether a white powdery substance is cocaine or baking soda. It determines the presence of specific drugs, blood, or gunpowder.

The test does not establish with certainty the presence of illegal drugs, but it does enable police to go forward with their investigation. Field tests should not be admissible into evidence since they are not scientifically reliable.

Narcotics Roadblocks (Drug Checkpoints)

Courts uphold the use of some narcotics traffic roadblocks which justify the use of suspicionless stops.

Agreeing that Interstates 70 and 44 are known drug trafficking routes, police are allowed to stop motorists on public highways in the absence of any particularized suspicion of crime. Police erect a sign that indicates: *Drug Checkpoint-One Mile Ahead.*

In fact, the sign is a ruse and there is no actual checkpoint. Instead, there is a turnoff or exit ramp located between the sign and the site of the supposed roadblock. The exit has no advertised services and there is normally a stop sign at the exit ramp.

Police then congregate, complete with drug detection dogs, approach your vehicle, and inquire as to why you exited the highway. They ask for permission to search your car. Whether you agree or not, they detain you and sic the dog on your vehicle. The rest is history, and you're toast.

When you see a drug checkpoint sign, do not pull off!

Courts reason that such checkpoints do not interfere with or intrude on most motorists, and that they are effective in advancing the state's interest in eliminating drugs. They require cops' questioning to be brief. National figures indicate that the average stop lasts two to three minutes, barring complications, with an overall "hit rate" of approximately nine percent. The fact is the roadblocks infringe upon the privacy of innocent citizens and is just another example of Big Brother.

Forfeiture Laws (Seize and Freeze)

Federal and state laws provide that any vehicle, boat, or plane that transports any quantity of drugs (the zero tolerance rule), plus any money, guns, or anything else of value in connection with drugs, be declared a public nuisance and forfeited to the government.

The *res* (thing) is seized by the police. An innocent owner or spouse can come forward to explain why he was unaware of the presence of drugs. The owner may claim the Fifth Amendment and refuse to answer, but he has little chance of getting his property returned.

A civil lawsuit is filed and then stayed until the criminal trial is complete. Interrogatories, depositions, and other discovery may occur so that each side can prepare for trial. The civil proceeding occurs whether or not the accused is ever convicted and is separate from the criminal trial.

Common defenses used to request property be returned include the following:

- The Defense of $8,850
- The Pearson Yacht Defense
- Duress, necessity, and impossibility
- Equitable estoppel
- Entrapment
- Stolen property defense
- deMinimis Defense
- Accused acquitted in the criminal case
- Innocent owner/spouse
- Proportionality test
- Double jeopardy

The Defense of $8,850 (undue government delay) is frequently used. In bringing lawsuits, the government sometimes delays and may have violated deadlines. Courts use the Barker-Wingo Balancing Test, which balances:

- The length of the delay
- The reason for the delay
- The defendant's assertion of his constitutional rights
- The prejudice to the defendant

Rule: **Always demand a speedy hearing in a forfeiture case and claim constitutional rights.**

In the Pearson Yacht Defense, you argue that if you have property stolen or taken from you without permission, it will serve no purpose to forfeit your property. If you claim to be an innocent owner, you have to prove that you took reasonable steps to prevent the criminal use of your property and that you had no advance knowledge your property was to be associated with drugs.

In the equitable estoppel defense, you argue that the government agent caused you to take a wrong action or failed to take action in time to avoid the forfeiture.

In the deMinimis defense, you argue that the drugs found were so small or that your car was so expensive or important to you that a forfeiture would be against public policy and be extremely harsh. It seems unfair to forfeit a $30,000 car if only a small residue of drugs was found (this is the proportionality argument).

Forfeiture laws enacted to combat drug scourges need to be drastically rewritten. The laws were aimed at big-time dealers. The idea is not to send them to jail but to deprive them of lavish possessions—fancy cars, yachts, and mansions—their illegal drug trade has allowed them to acquire. Instead, automobiles are being taken from casual drug users stopped for minor traffic violations.

A conviction isn't necessary before police can confiscate your car. Administrative seizures can be undertaken by the state and later adopted by the federal government. Whether you are ever convicted of any crime, the burden of proof is on you.

In state court, police must report the seizure within three days, and five days later the prosecutor must file a court petition. In federal court, authorities take plenty of time, advertise your name in *USA Today*, and presume that you are guilty.

Unless forfeiture laws are reformed, the nation's drug war will increasingly become a pretext for exploiting citizens. In the meantime, many are regularly being denied their constitutional rights.

Laundered Money (Dirty Dollars)

Automobile dealers, antique dealers, jewelers, pawnbrokers, lawyers, real estate and insurance agents—all may know something the government needs to know: who the big cash spenders are.

Each may be the recipient of requests to purchase services, products, or property with large amounts of cash. Large cash purchases are a way for drug dealers to hide sources and amounts.

The *1970 Bank Secrecy Act* and the *1984 Tax Reform Act* are intended to reduce the use of banks to launder money. Any business or person receiving more than $10,000 in cash from one customer must report all such transactions (IRS Form 8300) within fifteen days of the payment.

Defending Yourself Against a Drug Arrest

Places where drug arrests are most likely to occur are as follows:

- In your car after being stopped for a minor traffic violation
- Disembarking from a plane, bus, or train
- In your home while police are serving an arrest or search warrant
- While selling or buying drugs
- On interstate highways traveling from the West to the East Coast. Money couriers travel from east to west.

If you are traveling in a rental car that has an air freshener (to mask the smell of drugs) and out-of-state plates from a source state (Arizona, California, or another western state) and are headed eastbound toward St. Louis, Chicago, or Detroit, then police will separate you and the passenger and ask routine questions. They will inquire as to your destination and purpose, the length of your trip, and the contents of your vehicle. They will then compare notes, keeping you and your passenger separated, and decide that you have given inconsistent statements.

After asking whether you are carrying any guns or drugs, they ask for permission to look in your car, or sometimes for permission to search your car and its contents.

They should use written consent forms, but more than likely they'll ask only for oral consent. This sets up a factual situation where it is your word against theirs as to whether or not you consented. They will always win. If you insist on your constitutional rights and refuse permission to search, they will take this to mean that you are hiding something. If you give them consent to search, they will go ahead and search.

Their initial stop of your car will be on some minor traffic offense, such as failing to signal a lane change, weaving, or following too closely. It makes no difference as to why you're stopped—once stopped they will begin incessant questioning.

If you refuse the search, they use a drug-sniffing dog. If the dog makes an affirmative response on your vehicle, police consider this probable cause to search your vehicle whether or not you consent. Police will search your trunk, glove compartment, locked suitcase, or other closed areas.

Police have no absolute right to detain you on the shoulder of a highway and question you beyond the time reasonably necessary for the nonculpable traffic offense for which you have been stopped. There is no absolute duty of a citizen to jaw with police and answer every question asked.

> Rule: **Drive strictly within the law and avoid being stopped. If stopped, answer the officer politely, produce your operator's license, and say nothing more. Most citizens talk too much. Your mouth is your worst enemy. If asked about your destination or origination point, or the purpose and length of your trip, politely tell the officer you decline to be interrogated. If he has a traffic ticket to give you, then take it, as you do not wish to be detained further.**

Do not aid in supplying probable cause to search your vehicle. If he asks you to get out of the vehicle, comply. Do not respond to any other demands. If he demands the key to the trunk, suitcases, or glove box, or that you identify your luggage, you are not obligated to say or do anything except to respond, "Officer, am I under arrest? I wish to resume my journey." The less you say, the better.

If the officer searches and finds drugs, he may misquote or misunderstand anything you say. Once written in his report, it is etched in stone and will be used against you at trial. Rather than say something he might misinterpret as consent, an inconsistent statement, or confession, it is better to say nothing.

Most citizens believe if they are polite, kind, and cooperative, the officer will go away and they can somehow fool or trick him. Don't count on this!

If you are innocent and have no contraband, you should fully cooperate and be released. If you are carrying contraband, they will not leave you alone unless you fully cooperate or satisfy their desire to conduct a complete search. They are going to search you—legally or illegally.

If you decide not to cooperate, do not respond to their questions. They have to show probable cause to stop you and conduct a search. If you do not add fuel to the fire by giving inconsistent statements or stopping to give them an opportunity to observe other unusual things (such as suspicious bulges in your wearing apparel or luggage), they will have less legal proof to use in court.

If you are in your home or business and police knock on the door announcing their identity and purpose, you are not required to do or say anything. If you do not answer the door allowing them entrance, they have the right to knock down the door to gain entry.

You are not required to identify yourself, take police on a tour of your house, answer questions, or explain the contents in your house. Your best course of action is to sit down in the living room and shut up. The more you say, the deeper you will be mired in your own problems.

If you are in a parking lot, public street, or some other place where a drug purchase or sale has just transpired or you have committed a crime in the presence of an undercover law enforcement officer or wired informant, he has the right to immediately arrest you. But you do not have the right to a speedy arrest. If the officer or informant is undercover, he may have other cases to work and may not wish to reveal his identity because he is currently protecting his secrecy. He may go ahead and;make a drug buy from you then make his report to the prosecutor, but formal charges might not be filed for a year, or until the police have completed a number of other cases.

Drugs have to be chemically tested, and there may be a delay of several months at the crime laboratory. Once formal charges are filed, a warrant is issued for your arrest and police then come to your door to arrest you. In the process, attempting to get you to walk from room to room to get dressed and get your personal belongings, they may search rooms, closets, dresser drawers, and areas that you are near (in order to look for weapons that you might grab).

Don't keep contraband, guns, or large sums of cash in your home. If police serve an arrest warrant, they will make a limited protective sweep search and if items are observed in plain view, you will be charged with a new crime and your property will be seized and forfeited.

Rule: **When police serve an arrest or search warrant, yield to their demands and submit your person or property to a search. Do not argue with their authority. Claim your rights**

254

in taking the Fifth Amendment. Do not discuss the case unless you have had an opportunity to talk with a lawyer and get expert legal advice. Your lawyer can file a motion to suppress and question the validity of the search, and the judge will decide if the evidence should be used against you. You are not required to cooperate with police. Answering their questions and conducting them on a tour of your property is the common mistake made by most citizens trying to be polite. You are not required to speak, give consent, or do anything to help the police. They are going to arrest you and/or search your property anyway, so let them conduct their investigation without handing them your head on a platter.

Stings and Reverse Stings

Sometimes police work undercover and recruit confidential informants to infiltrate loose-knit gangs and groups. Police conduct sting operations, posing as gang members or businessmen buying stolen property or drugs, and engage in ongoing business with criminals until a case has been made. When an arrest is made, undercover cops reveal their identities.

A *reverse sting* is where police intercept drugs or stolen property in transit and get an informant to roll with the contraband and sell it to a criminal. *Reverse sting* means that the contraband is being sold rather than purchased.

Courts approve these police practices unless police become involved in the criminal activity, engage in criminal misconduct, or use entrapment. Police usually videotape or audiotape the buys.

CHAPTER 12

A Trip to the Can

"I may hate sin, but never the sinner."
—CLARENCE DARROW (1857-1938)

"In my twenties, I was my own moral authority. The inadequacies of that ... are painfully obvious today."
—DR. LAURA SCHLESSINGER (1947-)

Despite your best efforts, sometimes it is impossible to avoid being convicted and going to prison. Discretion may be the better part of valor, and a negotiated plea of guilty maybe your best course of action.

In state prisons, only a small percentage of most prison terms must actually be served behind bars (unless you are sentenced as a persistent or dangerous offender). A higher percentage of time (eighty-five percent) must be served in federal prisons, but the conditions are much nicer. Neither prison is a Holiday Inn.

If you are going to prison, you get credit for good time (no write-ups or disciplinary problems in prison) and back time (any time you served at the original time of arrest). You may be eligible for early release to a halfway house or house arrest. These are meaningful possibilities toward the end of your prison term.

While in prison, do the following:

1. Keep yourself meaningfully busy, physically and mentally occupied.
2. Volunteer for every job imaginable.
3. Enroll and successfully complete high school and college courses, earning GED and college credits.
4. Attend and participate in every self-improvement program offered, whether you think you need to or not, including drug and alcohol intervention.
5. Become a trusty.
6. Stay out of gangs, cliques, groups, and fights.
7. Keep to yourself.

Your release date may be placed far off, but eventually moved up. In state court, upon formal sentencing you go to the county jail and wait for the sheriff to transport you to Fulton, Missouri, to be tested, classified, and eventually assigned by the Department of Corrections (DOC) to one of a dozen state prisons.

In federal court, the prison location is designated by the Bureau of Prisons (BOP) after sentencing. Your lawyer will ask for permission for you to personally report to the institution, which places you in a lower security risk category and gives you more freedom and benefits.

Getting Ready for Prison

For first-time offenders, facing the reality of incarceration can be a daunting prospect. Many have lived privileged lives, possess good educations, and know nothing of the confines and restraints of fortressed walls.

It is a challenge for the criminal defense lawyer to prepare his client for the venture into the uncertainties of life in state or federal prison. Most criminal defense attorneys are really not familiar with navigating such government bureaucracy.

You must be prepared for the interview with the probation officer. The most important item that will ever be written about you is the

Presentence Investigation (PSI). Yet most attorneys place little emphasis on attempting to affect this broad-sweeping document which follows an inmate through his entire period of incarceration, including a halfway house and probation periods. The PSI can determine how you will be treated in prison, to what facility you will be assigned, and even what type of work assignment you will receive.

In federal court, determining your eligibility for the SOO-hour Comprehensive Drug and Alcohol Abuse Program (DAP) or the Intensive Confinement Center Program is important since it reduces your sentence one year.

A request for specific prison facilities can also be a critical decision, although there are no guarantees. Some facilities offer college and graduate degrees, better meals, or facilities.

Knowing how to behave in prison is important. Some inmates arrive with laptops, cell phones, designer jogging suits, and $150 running shoes. Conjugal visits are not on the itinerary.

Expect to receive a Dear John letter from your significant other. Engage in activities that keep you stimulated and busy. Boredom is the worst part of being locked up. According to author, lecturer, and former convict Ronald A. Cohen, who operates a client advisory group and owns a business that consults with prospective prisoners, the torture in prison exists in the agonizing monotony of daily life.

What to Wear

Don't wear a suit to jail—it's inappropriate and identifies you as a member of a group. Stay out of groups or cliques. Dress inconspicuously and select clothing which will be comfortable.

Wear shoes with Velcro straps (instead of laces) or loafers, since they'll take your shoelaces once you get to jail, along with your belt or anything else they think is a safety hazard.

Use the "layered look." Jail temperatures are rarely comfortable and change as more people get stuffed into cells or as guards open windows. Wear several T-shirts underneath a flannel shirt, a pair of jeans, and thick socks.

Choose your time of surrender well. Don't surrender on a Friday night when all the violent drunks are coming in. Surrender midmorning on Tuesday through Thursday. On Monday people are grumpy. By Tuesday, they've resigned themselves to the week and will be nicer to you.

The Reception Center

Sounds cozy, doesn't it? Almost like they're serving coffee and doughnuts. Wrong.

The reception center is where you'll be made fully aware that you're captive. You've been to jail, now you're going to prison. You'll be shipped in chains. Your hands are cuffed, your feet are chained together, and another chain links you to other prisoners.

After arrival your hair will be sheared. You'll be stripped naked and your clothes will be taken away. You'll bend over and spread your cheeks so a guard can peek or poke a finger.

The degradation is complete and deliberate. Swallow all your anger, embarrassment, and pride. Resistance is futile. You'll be herded through a fast shower, sprayed with insecticide, and given an ill-fitting uniform.

The reception center will give you some orientation to prison life while it is determined which facility is be best suited for you. You are severed once and for all from society, and the intensity of the hate, fear, and sadness is palpable. The world is bleak and horrid. You'll hear men crying and there will be no compassion for your situation.

Prison Rape

Of all the fears men have about prison, this is the worst. Loss of liberty, bad food, loneliness, claustrophobia—none of them compare to the prospect of being raped. Wardens and guards may deny that it happens, give ludicrous explanations, or blame the victim for making a mistake in judgment and hanging out with the wrong crowd.

Homosexuality is not something that even prisoners like to admit. They know rape is animalistic and won't acknowledge that it happens. To the simple question, "Am I going to get raped?" the answer is, "Probably." Conservative estimates indicate that at least thirty thousand males are sexually assaulted every year in prisons and jails.

Gay men in prison are the most vulnerable to rape and will be beaten and raped as often as is necessary until they seek protection. They become "punks" and their lives will be worse than wretched for the rest of their term in prison.

Domination is the name of the game. The man screwing the punk is "pitching" and not "catching." Kindness is taken as a weakness in prison. Some guys choose to be a punk as a way of surviving until their sentence is finished.

The sight of a man being abused beyond his ability to withstand it is offensive. Once the transformation takes place, there is no turning back. Never show that you're scared.

Never borrow or accept anything from strangers. Don't refuse in a scared way, but don't try to act tough. Don't try to be friends with everyone or stay off in your cell like a coward. If anyone tries to "punk" you, don't be cowed or intimidated. Stand up for your rights.

If you must, don't hesitate to fight. If you have to live in prison for any length of time, you may as well do it on your own terms and not as somebody's slave. If it comes to a confrontation, fight to win. Your first impression will be a lasting one that you must live with.

Be observant of your surroundings. Don't meddle in others' business. Chose your associates carefully.

Sentencing

"Experience is the name everyone gives to their mistakes."
—OSCAR WILDE (1854-1900)

"Violence is as American as apple pie."
—H. RAPP BROWN (1943-)

Many people are willing to change, not because they see the light, but because they feel the heat.

Possible sentences include imprisonment, fine, probation ("paper"), house arrest, suspended imposition of sentence, and "shock" probation, where you are sent to jail for a few days to get a taste of incarceration before you go home and begin a term of probation.

If a fine is assessed, the money goes to the school fund. If you're sentenced in city or municipal court it goes to city revenue.

Before you enter a plea, consider the facts of the case, your reason for entering the plea, and whether y u are in fact guilty. You are advised of the range of punishment and other important constitutional rights.

If a Sentencing Assessment Report (SAR) has been requested, you have the right to contradict any part you believe is false. If a plea bargain has been entered into, the court is not obligated to accept the bargain. If the judge does not accept the plea bargain, he gives you an opportunity to withdraw your plea. The prosecutor agrees only to recommend a certain sentence to the judge, which is not a guarantee that you will actually receive that sentence.

You may be given a suspended imposition of sentence, which means no sentence is actually imposed after the guilty plea and the court actually takes the matter under advisement for a period of time. If you succeed on probation, then the conviction is erased from your record. The file is closed under the Missouri Sunshine Law.

Plea bargaining is a proper procedure in which the court does not usually participate. The court will disclose whether or not it will follow the agreement.

After sentencing, the trial judge asks questions to determine whether there is probable cause to believe that you did not receive effective assistance from your lawyer.

Post-Trial Matters

"It ain't over until it's over."
—Yogi Berra (1947-)
New York Yankees

A prisoner may petition the trial court to set aside the conviction if the conviction or plea was caused by a denial of some constitutional right.

Grounds for successful motions include the following:

- Ineffective assistance of counsel
- Involuntary waiver of jury trial
- Denial of right to confront witnesses
- Incompetence to stand trial
- Forced confession
- Conviction based on perjured testimony
- Double jeopardy
- Insufficiency of criminal charge
- Unconstitutional identification
- Use of improper prior conviction
- Involuntary abandonment of right of appeal
- Failure of the lawyer to properly investigate facts
- Improper actions of the prosecutor

Unsuccessful grounds include the following:

- Matters raised on prior motion
- Matters already decided on appeal
- Matters waived on appeal
- Failure to allege sufficient facts
- Illegal arrest
- Unlawful search or seizure
- Newly discovered evidence
- Lack of speedy trial
- Failure to give *Miranda* warnings
- Dissatisfaction with penal conditions
- Irregularities at preliminary hearing
- Illegal evidence, confession, insanity, entrapment
- Imperfect criminal charge
- Trial errors
- Errors in admission of evidence
- Cruel or unusual punishment

You must file a motion for a new trial alleging specific trial errors. An appeal can include only those matters contained in the motion, or those that constitute plain error and result in a manifest injustice. You can file a writ of habeas corpus alleging an unconstitutional deprivation of freedom, but you won't win.

State Court Postconviction Motions

There are two procedures by which you can return to court to contest your imprisonment:

Rule 24.035

After a *plea of guilty,* if you are sentenced to imprisonment and claim the plea was involuntarily entered, your attorney was *ineffective,* or the sentence was illegal, you can file one postconviction motion (PCM). You must state all grounds known to you and raise every claim to challenge your sentence.

Rule 29.15

After a *trial,* if you believe that your lawyer was incompetent, that illegal evidence was used against you, or that the trial judge made serious errors, you may file one post-trial motion to attack your conviction. You must be in custody and actually serving time in prison.

Postconviction motions must be filed within ninety days after you enter prison and may be amended one time after a lawyer makes an entry of appearance or a public defender is appointed.

The court will make a preliminary finding as to whether an evidentiary hearing is required on the motion, and if not, may summarily refuse to hear prisoner's arguments. The judge may order a hearing in which testimony is heard.

Rule: **The object of postconviction remedies is to discover those relatively few cases in which an inmate has suffered a genuine deprivation of his constitutional rights. Your chances of success are not good.**

Pardons and Paroles

A pardon can be granted only by the governor and is an act of grace.

A judicial parole is a conditional release with the objective of rehabilitating the prisoner. A judge can grant only two paroles for anyone crime. A parole comes only after judgment and sentencing. A court can revoke a parole within the time period of the original sentence. Any convicted felon can be paroled or given a suspended imposition of sentence, or the judge may actually pronounce sentence and suspend it under any conditions, including shock probation.

The State Board of Probation and Parole has authority to hear parole applications for prisoners and conducts all pardon investigations. The board considers employment, social history, attitude, criminal record, conduct, and the best interests of society.

Court parole violation warrants are bondable. At the hearing, reliable hearsay evidence may be received. You should be represented by counsel. If the violations are admitted, no hearing is necessary.

Punishments

Missouri has the following punishments:

- Capital murder—life imprisonment or death
- Class A felony—ten to thirty years imprisonment, or life
- Class B felony—five to fifteen years imprisonment
- Class C felony—maximum seven years imprisonment, or up to one year and $5,000
- Class D felony—maximum five years imprisonment, or up to one year and $5,000
- Class A misdemeanor—six months to one year in jail, or fine of up to $1,000
- Class B misdemeanor—thirty days in jail or less, fine of up to $300
- Infraction—no jail, fine of up to $200, except where a person has derived economic gain

A judge may sentence you to an extended term of imprisonment if you are a persistent or dangerous offender and have a prior felony record.

On any felony conviction there is a conditional release, which includes the maximum of the entire prison sentence which also may be extended.

Many prisoners are expected to serve 120 days in prison. Upon successful completion you are then released by the Judge unless it is found to be an "abuse of discretion."

Missouri now has nine specific crimes affectionately known as the "nine deadly sins" in which upon conviction you must serve 85 percent of the assessed prison term.

120-Day Call-Back

The judge retains jurisdiction of your case for up to 120 days from the date that you enter the prison. He can order a report from the prison to see whether you are a suitable candidate for a 120-day callback. If so, he can order you to be released from prison. This authority rests solely with the judge. You may not petition for the 120-day probation. It is granted as an act of mercy by him, although an enterprising attorney can present helpful information to the judge as to why his client deserves parole. If paroled, you are under supervised probation of the State Board of Parole and Probation and the circuit judge.

If you do not obtain a 120-day probation call-back, you serve as much of the sentence as the State Department of Corrections desires. Despite salient factor scores and other regulations, only God knows how long you'll serve. If your crime was drug-or alcohol-related and did not involve violence, you can ask the court to reduce the sentence.

If you commit a violation after you have been released from prison, the probation officer can place you in jail without bond and the Department of Corrections will decide whether you are to be returned to prison. If you are paroled under the 120-day law, the trial judge decides whether your parole is to be revoked.

Remember, when you are on parole or probation, you are a second-class citizen. You're not allowed to violate any law. You cannot possess firearms or associate with convicted felons and must report all changes of address, employment, and marital status within hours. Any parolee who refuses to do these things is a fool and is asking for a one-way ticket back to prison. Get the chip off your shoulder. If you think you have any constitutional rights, try getting caught littering or spitting on the sidewalk.

You are eligible for house arrest in which you wear a monitoring device on your leg that requires you to keep stringent curfews.

It is important to attend all useful and constructive classes and programs offered in prison. Obtain your high school equivalency degree. Attend college courses, Alcoholics Anonymous, Narcotics Anonymous, sexual offender programs, and counseling and therapy sessions. Volunteer for work details, regardless of whether you think you need them.

Whenever possible, you will want to make trusty status by indicating your hard work, good faith, and sincere desire and efforts to improve yourself. If you have any pending criminal charges or detainers, demand speedy disposition of those detainers.

Parole Hearings

**Success consists of getting up just one more time
than you've fallen down.**

Depending upon your prior felony record, you will be eligible for parole after serving approximately one-third of your state prison time. A parole board hearing will be held where you are given a few precious minutes to state why you believe you are ready to return to society. You're entitled to have a friend, relative, or attorney present with you at the hearing, which is tape recorded. Be prepared for the victim to be present.

Rule: **The mistake most prisoners make is to try to minimize or explain away their crime—a sure sign you are not remorseful and have not accepted responsibility. Your best bet is to admit the past, accept responsibility, and be positive about the future. What are your plans for the future, your home, employment, and church upon your release? The parole board** does not want to be embarrassed by a new parolee immediately committing another crime.

Rule: At parole hearings, as at sentencing hearings, always present a brochure or scrapbook with photographs of your family, home, future employer, and church, as well as certificates, awards, and degrees that you might have earned, together with numerous good character letters. This brochure will get the attention of the judge or parole board and might tip the scales enough for you to be granted parole.

Habeas Corpus

A writ of habeas corpus (Latin for *you have the body*) is a command by a judge to have a person held in custody and then brought before the court for the purpose of determining the legality of confinement. Without this guarantee, police could take the people into custody and keep them there indefinitely. When the Bastille was stormed during the French Revolution, men were set free who had been imprisoned without trial for years. The writ protects against such actions and can be suspended in the event of rebellion or invasion, or when public safety might require it. Only twice in our nation's history (during the Civil War and in Hawaii during World War II) was the writ suspended.

Jailhouse Lawyers

You have the right to file lawsuits on your own behalf. Johnson v. Avery (1969) ruled it was your right to receive free access to someone with training in the law. Prisoners may file *pro se* or *impropria persona* (for himself) lawsuits. Most of these are frivolous and poorly written, and they rarely succeed. They work for cigarettes and other favors. Always remember, you get what you pay for.

Prisons: The Punishing Cost

Every week, like clockwork, the total number of prison inmates grows. The average inmate costs $30,000 a year to feed, house, and guard. With over two million behind bars in state and federal prisons, the United States already has the highest incarceration rate in the western world—four times the per capita rate of England or France.

Legislators are afraid to complain about spiraling costs lest they be labeled soft on crime. Nobody wants to be accused of being a wimp. Everyone wants to act tough, and toughness is translated into longer sentences. Sooner or later you have to ask whether you are willing to let your kid have a mediocre education in order to send a few more people to prison.

The opposite view is that while it may cost thousands to keep a man behind bars, it may cost as much as $430,000 yearly to let that man run free, committing crimes. This figure is based on the idea that criminals in prison would each commit 187 crimes a year if they were running free, and the average crime costs society about $2,300.

Less than one percent of all crime results in a prison sentence, so even doubling or tripling the incarceration rate has little real impact on crime.

What about rehabilitation? Overstretched budgets and terrible crowding in most prisons preclude all but the most minimal rehabilitative efforts. Worse, prisons often unwittingly function as graduate schools for crime.

Halfway houses, work release, and community service provide regular counseling and supervision without the expense of constant guarding and concrete walls and may be the answer of the twenty-first century. At sentencings, judges must be convinced to use them, saving the state money and giving offenders a chance to re-enter society in a controlled way.

Prisoners Pay for Jail Upkeep

Prisoners who have sufficient assets and money have to pay some of the costs of their incarceration under the Missouri Incarceration Reimbursement Act. The law empowers the state attorney general to collect thousands of dollars per prisoner toward the cost of the inmate's incarceration.

In the Presentence Investigation, information is gathered about financial assets and given to the Attorney General. Assets seized and collected are assigned to the state Department of Corrections. This includes workmen's compensation, pension benefits, previously earned wages, bonuses, annuities, retirement benefits, settlements, claims against the state, or judgments received by the prisoners against a state officer. Exempt assets include homes and an inmate's wages up to $2,500.

The prisoner is given thirty days' notice before his case is heard by the court, and the state may not recover more than ninety percent of the value of the prisoner's assets.

The judge can assess reasonable costs of the county jail, which the inmate must pay. In other words, you have to pay for doing jail time.

Overcrowding at Federal Prisons

Federal prisons are now at 150 percent capacity. Nearly sixty percent of all prisoners are confined on drug-related crimes.

An impact can be made on crime through rehabilitation, since eventually the prisoner will be released into society. Rehabilitation includes the following steps:

- Every federal prisoner is required to have a high school diploma before he can take part in any preferred federal prison program.
- *Drug treatment* programs are now required.
- Every federal prisoner must work. Prison industries employ thousands of prisoners each day.
- Boot camp.
- Home confinement (house arrest).

Recidivism

About fifty percent of all prisoners are back in prison within three years. People can change, but often they don't want to change, or are not getting the help to make the change. Our goal should be to keep people permanently out of prison and provide a successful and corrective environment the first time.

Prisoners need real-world contacts—help from people on the outside to show an interest or to make a call on a prisoner's behalf.

World's Top Jailer

"There are seven million laws in this country, and I intend to break everyone, including the law of gravity."
—Abbie Hoffman 0936-1989)

"It is not the beginning of the end, and it is certainly not the end, but it may be the end of the beginning."
—Sir Winston Churchill
(1874-1965)

Our prison system overflows with two million inmates in 3,320 jails. While inmate population has increased, so has violent crime. The cost to incarcerate inmates is over $20 billion each year, or $30,000 per inmate, which is about the same as the cost of a college education.

Innovation and alternative sentencing should be used. One useful approach is house arrest—jailing low-risk prisoners at home where they are electronically monitored at less than one-fourth of the cost of prison. They can work and support themselves, but their activity is restricted. Other approaches are halfway houses, drug and alcohol treatment programs, and community service—performing good works to pay back the community. That's smarter than being the world's top jailer.

Our system tries to control criminals and tries to provide for equal protection of our citizens. Americans believe that our country is soft on crime. This is not true. We have the longest prison sentences in the free world and the highest per-capita prison population in the entire world. We are the planet's most imprisoned people.

Women Behind Bars

There are seventeen men doing time for every female prisoner. The reason for this ratio can be boiled down to drugs and testosterone.

About fifty percent of all women in federal prisons have been convicted of drug-related offenses. Other crimes, such as theft, armed robbery, bad checks, and prostitution, are also drug-related.

270

Eighty percent of all women entering prisons are mothers; most have custody of their children. The number of women inmates has tripled in the past ten years. They face a system designed and run by men for men. By contrast, only sixty percent of male prisoners are fathers, and less than half have any custodial responsibility.

What You Need to Know About a Criminal Conviction

Being a convicted felon is serious business and has many collateral consequences.

If you're convicted of a felony, you lose certain federal and state benefits. A person convicted of distribution of drugs can be ineligible for federal benefits for up to five years for the first offense, and forever on a third and subsequent offense. Federal benefits mean any grant, contract, loan, professional license, or commercial license provided by any agency of the United States.

The Immigration and Naturalization Service (INS) considers drug enforcement a high priority. There is substantial likelihood that any drug conviction of a noncitizen will come to the attention of the INS. An immigrant can be deported for being a drug addict, whether or not he is convicted. Say goodbye to your passport.

You lose your right to vote (disenfranchisement) as the county clerk removes your name from voter rolls. You are forbidden to own or legally possess a firearm while on probation. Convicted felons lose their operator's license if a motor vehicle was used in their crime. You are severely limited in obtaining any licenses from the state (nurses, doctors, lawyers, accountants, real estate or insurance agents, barbers).

If you become a cooperating witness, however, a denial of federal benefits may not apply.

Sentencing in Federal Court

The Federal Sentencing Guidelines divide all federal crimes into forty-three levels of seriousness and set base sentences. To determine these, the Sentencing Commission used a pool of ten thousand past convictions and averaged out the actual time served for each category of crime. The base sentence can be ratcheted up and down by an array of offense characteristics, such as the amount of money stolen or drugs possessed.

Tough sentencing laws in federal court require almost any convicted felon to actually do time in a federal penitentiary. If you cooperate with the federal prosecutor by agreeing to testify against others, you do have a chance for probation, house arrest, home detention, or confinement at a halfway house.

The Commission sets up guideline ranges from which the judge may select a sentence, although under certain circumstances the judge may depart up or depart down from the guidelines. The purpose of the law is to have an effective and fair sentencing system with honesty, uniformity, and proportionality. The sentence depends upon the criminal history of the defendant, whether a weapon was used, the amount of property stolen or damage done, and hundreds of other factors and categories in order to determine the appropriate punishment. The punishment is scaled to offenders' culpability and the resulting harms.

The law requires the judge to consider:

1. The nature of the offense
2. The history and characteristics of the offender
3. The kinds of sentences available
4. The guidelines and policy statements of the Commission
5. The need to avoid unwarranted disparity
6. The need for the sentence to serve the purposes of deterrent, incapacitation, rehabilitation, and retribution

There are a large number of relevant factors that determine the guideline range, including whether your acts were intentional, reckless, or merely negligent, as well as your state of mind, which has bearing on your intent, motive, and purpose in committing the crime.

Federal sentencing is extremely complicated, and your attorney must be a skilled expert. A creative defense attorney has a number of grounds he can argue for a downward departure from the guidelines.

These relate to his client's youthfulness, unique family upbringing, exceptional military service, diminished mental capacity, motive for committing the offense, and a number of other factors.

Once you're sentenced, the U.S. Attorney can file a Rule 35 motion asking your sentence be reduced on the grounds of cooperation and assistance to the government. It is rarely done so don't count on it.

Plea bargain agreements are where the government and defendant enter into an agreement as to what is going to be said to the judge, what the recommendations are on sentencing, and other matters.

You may be allowed to submit an Alford plea. This means you tell the judge you really did not do the act in question, but you plead guilty because the facts are such that the jury would be likely to convict you.

Getting into Club Fed

Throughout the United States there are *Regional Designators* who coordinate placement of newly sentenced defendants and assign them to federal prisons. The designators hide in offices in faraway places. Forget trying to contact them. They seldom answer phone calls or mail.

The Regional Designator will consider:

1. Your past criminal record
2. Whether you've ever been confined in a prison
3. The seriousness of your crime
4. Whether you are considered violent
5. The location of family and friends who would be visiting you
6. Whether you have a skill or trade that might be used within the prison system
7. The availability of bed space

If the sentencing judge recommends you be confined in a particular prison, some weight will be given to the judge's wishes. The defense lawyer can provide information to the Regional Designator to make it more likely that you will be confined in a low-security prison near your home. This can make your stay in prison more convenient

273

and enjoyable than you might expect.

Some federal prisons are designated as *camps*. Inmates in these prisons are given more freedom, and confinement there is somewhat akin to being in military service. The higher-security prisons have regular daily countdowns. You have little or no freedom outside your cell and are confined in small spaces with dangerous, violent prisoners. These prisons are a living hell and should be avoided at all costs.

Son of Sam Laws

Recent laws stipulate that the proceeds of true-crime stories should benefit victims of crime rather than the perpetrators. These "Son of Sam" laws reflect a compelling state interest in taking away the fruits of crime from criminals. The laws are named after serial killer David Berkowitz, known as the Son of Sam, who terrorized New York City in 1977.

No criminal can profit from the proceeds of the sale of a book or movie. The money must be paid over to a state agency to be held in escrow in case the victim decides to file suit.

Tips for Prisoners

1. Accept that you have lost control of your life and are living a structured, repetitive lifestyle.
2. Mind your own business. Don't try to win a popularity contest.
3. Obey the rules. Don't get crosswise with staff members.
4. Park your prejudices at the front door.
5. If you get a Dear John letter from a spouse or significant other, accept it and move on. Be your own best friend.
6. Stay as busy as possible. No pity parties.
7. Prison food is not half bad.

—COMPLIMENTS OF RON COHEN
The Client Advisory Group,
Addison, Texas

Inside of a ring or out, ain't nothing wrong with going down. It's staying down that's wrong.
—Cassius Clay, a/k/a
Muhammed Ali

Be very careful, then, how you live-not as unwise but as wise, making the most of every moment, because the days are evil. Therefore, do not be foolish, but understand what the Lord's will is.
—Ephesians 5: 15-17 NIV

Free Legal Advice

"Test everything. Hold on to the good. Avoid every kind of evil."
—1 Thessalonians 5:21—22

"To no one will we sell, to no one will we refuse or delay right or justice."
—Magna Carta, 1215

People ask, "Why do crime rates continue to soar? What can be done about the drug war? What are the reasons for increased teenage pregnancies and juvenile delinquency?" The answer: *The breakdown of the family unit by moral decay.*

Children everywhere are neglected, without encouragement or praise. More than fifty percent of Americans live in family units missing either a mother or father. Teenagers watch thousands of hours of television trash which condone violence, pornography, and perverted lifestyles.

The problem will get much worse before it gets better. Until we reclaim the streets, return to church, and revamp the liberal mentality ("If it feels good, do it"), crime as a social problem and a multibillion-dollar expense will continue to mount.

"We have lost our moral compass. There are lots of ways to control crime. The first way is the home and the neighborhood.

The second way is to warehouse criminals. This carries an enormous cost, and when the person gets out of prison they are worthless. We are losing a generation of people."
—Chief Justice Gerald T. Joflat
United States Court of Appeals

We have lost faith in our ability to take care of ourselves and each other. We have relegated the problem to the police, the courts, and social welfare agencies. The crime problem is too important to be left just to them.

Rule: **Combating crime is the business of every American. None of us can afford to abdicate our personal responsibility. The criminal justice system cannot guarantee our well-being any more than physicians can guarantee our health. Each of us must take primary responsibility for his health with doctors as backup consultants. Each of us must take primary responsibility for his own safety, with the police called upon as little as possible.**

Conclusion

You want to go about your business free from fear that you will be assaulted or robbed. You want your family to be safe on the streets or at home and to retire at night knowing that they are not in danger.

The criminal law, whose primary function is to protect us from the criminal, must get on with its task. Some say we will never remedy the problem of crime unless we defeat poverty, ignorance, and racial prejudice as the ultimate causes. Those who earnestly advance this argument never explain why a vast amount of crime is committed by people who are neither poor nor unintelligent, nor have ever suffered a day of racial discrimination. We cannot wait until we have rebuilt society according to some utopian reformists' prescription before dealing with the all-too-commonplace, everyday savagery of crime.

Willie "The Actor" Sutton, the dapper and ingenious bank robber whose exploits in the '40s and '50s put him on the front pages, was examined by sociologists, criminologists, and psychiatrists. After they pinched, poked, and prodded every aspect of his life from toilet training on, with the assumption that Willie was somehow abnormal or had some particular genetic defect or environmental experience that compelled him to pursue a criminal career, he was asked, "Why do you rob banks?" Without a moment's hesitation Willie shot back: "Because that's where the money is."

We must avoid the tendency to regard crime as a form of mental illness. This is just a humanitarian disguise for the belief that we should not be held accountable for our acts. The criminal will go on planning and committing crimes as long as he thinks the law is weak and yielding enough to give him a chance to evade it.

If you're considering committing a crime—don't! It is wrong, and it isn't worth it. The cost of lawyers, bail bonds, and expenses is great. The embarrassment among friends and family will last a lifetime. The inhumanity of jail and prison is a nightmare.

We live in a Godless philosophy of moral relativism, dominant in America because parents allow it to exist, professors teach it, and churches passively accept it. The only politically correct way to think is that immorality may be moral, traditional concepts of right and wrong are passe, and everything comes in shades of gray. This philosophy strips life of its only source of meaning, since there are no absolute moral laws to contend with, and no God who promises to punish sin and hold us accountable. We are left in life to grope our way in search of monetary thrills and pleasures.

The message we must teach children in the twenty-first century is that they will be bombarded with moral relativism each day. But ultimately, God will require each of us to know the right answer. We will all face our own judgment day. The tide of relativism has invaded the classroom, from the elementary school to the university.

The United States wins its case whenever justice is done one of its citizens in the courts.

—Inscription on Department of
Justice Headquarters Building,
Washington, D.C.

"Everyone thinks of changing the world, but no one thinks of changing himself."
—LEO TOLSTOI (1828-1910)

"I could have accomplished three times what I accomplished. I haven't realized my full potential. It's disgusting."
—KATHERINE HEPBURN (1920-2003)
Movie Actress

Common Questions

What should I do when I am signaled to pull over?

Pull over to the side of the road as quickly and safely as possible, remain in your vehicle, and get ready to produce your driver's license and insurance papers, putting them in your hand while holding the upper part of the wheel. Stay composed, ask why you were stopped, and be polite.

Suppose the officer wants to search my car. Can he do so legitimately without a warrant?

Ask why the officer wants to conduct a search. You do not have to consent; and the officer may not search unless you do consent or the officer otherwise has probable cause. Ask the officer if you're under arrest, and if so, ask for an explanation. Don't interfere, as you can always challenge the legitimacy of the search later in court. Whether he can search depends upon the circumstances.

What part of my car may police search if they have probable cause? Does it include the glove compartment and closed containers?

Yes. The Supreme Court (under the automobile exception to the Fourth Amendment's protection against warrantless searches) allows such a search. The glove compartment and closed containers in the passenger compartment are subject to search.

Can police pull me over in a roadblock, demand to check my license, and question me?

Roadblocks do not constitute an unreasonable search as long as police stop all cars passing through the roadblock and follow a neutral policy.

What should I do if the police arrest me?

It is better to discuss what you should not do. Do not:

1. Speak to anyone else about your case
2. Answer police questions or waive your right to a lawyer
3. Submit to a lineup of any kind or test without your lawyer
4. Dodge news photographers or cover your face
5. Be impolite

What do I tell my lawyer while I'm in custody?

Be prepared to tell your attorney where the police have taken you, where the arrest occurred, what the charges are against you, and the amount of the bail.

Do not tell your lawyer anything else. Only answer his questions with "yes" or "no" answers since the police are listening to you on your end of the telephone line.

If my Missouri license has been revoked, can I go to another state and drive?

No. All other states recognize Missouri's law under the Full Faith and Credit Clause of the United States Constitution. Once your driving privilege has been revoked in one state, canceled, or suspended, then you cannot legally drive in any other state. If you obtain a driver's license in that state, you may be committing perjury.

What are the grounds for license suspension?

If you get three moving violations within one year in Missouri, refuse to submit to a breath testing device, or have an accident and fail to post insurance or a cost deposit with the Missouri Department of Revenue, you can lose your license for one year.

How long may police hold a suspect before filing charges?

If you are arrested on probable cause to believe you have committed a crime but yet no formal charges have been filed, you may be detained for up to twenty hours in the city or county jail. You may be able to make a PC (probable cause) bond and be freed during the twenty-hour period.

After this period of time, police must release you or bring formal charges and take you before a judge for arraignment.

What do I do if arrested for drunk driving?

Do not talk. Ask to speak to an attorney before you say something that will be used against you. Police are trained to gather information from you that will enable the prosecutor to convict you.

Should I perform the field sobriety tests?

No! These tests are designed to prove that you are intoxicated. If a police officer smells intoxicating liquor, no matter what you do or say, expect a request to submit to a breath test.

Just exactly how does a breath testing device work?

A sample of your lung air is analyzed by an infrared light beam, which a software-controlled computer transforms into your blood alcohol level.

Should I take a breath test?

Each case is different. You are allowed twenty minutes to telephone an attorney for advice on this question. Remember that you must request to speak to an attorney.

What kind of penalty am I likely to get for a DWI?

Up to 180 days in jail and a $500 fine is the maximum punishment for your first DWI. However, jail time is not usually imposed. An attorney may advise you about alternative approaches and options.

You can expect up to 365 days in jail and a $1,000 fine for a second DWI. You will serve two to seven days in jail for shock time.

What is the difference if the state suspends, revokes, or denies my license?

A suspension is for a period of thirty, sixty, or ninety days. A revocation is for one year and requires that you retest to regain your driver's license. A denial is for a period of five or ten years due to repeat DWIs.

I just got a speeding ticket. Should I hire a lawyer? Isn't it much cheaper just to plead guilty and pay a fine?

Yes, hire a lawyer. The attorney can save you time and money by appearing for you in court. Usually the ticket can be handled in a manner so that you will not lose your license for point violations and your insurance company will not raise your rates.

May the police use information from a confidential informant to obtain a search or arrest warrant?

The law allows police to use information if it is reliable. People often supply information to the police without having their identities disclosed. Police use this and other information to prove that the informant is reliable and that evidence from other sources confirms the informant's story.

If the judge determines that there is probable cause to believe the evidence, a search warrant will be issued. It must be served within ten days, and a photocopy of the search warrant and receipt must be left at the scene.

The search warrant affidavit is not required to be left, and it remains in the court file. This is the most important document and will explain to you all of the reasons the police have for believing that the evidence will be found at the location.

What procedures must police follow while making an arrest?

The police do not have to tell you the crime for which you are being arrested, although they probably will. They are not permitted to use excessive force. If you resist arrest, however, the police will use reasonable force to subdue you and keep you from injuring yourself.

Police are not required to advise you of your *Miranda* warning rights. Only if they intend to interrogate you do those rights have to be read and a waiver obtained.

When am I in custody?

You do not have to be placed *under arrest* in any formal manner. The law considers you in custody when you have been arrested or otherwise deprived of your freedom of movement in any significant way. This may occur when an officer is holding you at gunpoint, when other officers surround you, or when you have been handcuffed or placed in the back seat of a car. The most obvious example of being in custody is when the police say, "You are under arrest."

It does not matter if the police make an error and you are not subsequently charged with that specific crime, particularly as long as the officer acts in good faith.

What is an interrogation?

An interrogation may be explicit questioning such as "Did you kill John Doe?" or less obvious comments likely to elicit incriminating information from you.

If officers make comments, either directed to you or in your presence, that might be considered indirect questioning or the functional equivalent of questioning, it qualifies as an interrogation. Your *Miranda* rights must be scrupulously honored.

How do police recommend that criminal charges be filed against someone?

Criminal cases go through a screening process before an accused faces charges.

The two-step process begins with the police inquiry where the officers determine, in their own minds, if there's enough evidence to recommend the filing of charges. If not, the police release the arrested person from jail.

If the officer decides to recommend prosecution, he will take his reports to a prosecutor for review. The prosecutor may request follow-up investigation and alone will decide whether to file charges and what charges to allege.

These charges are then written in a complaint and filed with the court clerk's office.

When do I have the right to an attorney?

You have an absolute right to counsel before police questioning. Even before you are read your *Miranda* warning rights, you can tell police that you want a lawyer or do not wish to answer any questions until consulting with your attorney.

Once you ask for an attorney—stick with it! Don't give in to any questioning until you've talked with an attorney.

How long can I be held in jail?

Once you are arrested on probable cause by a law enforcement officer, Missouri allows you to be held no longer than twenty hours. The U.S. Supreme Court has recently declared that a person can be held a reasonable period of time until brought before a judge for arraignment.

During the twenty-hour period, you have the right to make a probable cause bond. If formal charges are not filed upon you within this period, police must arrest you, or they will be liable under civil tort law for false imprisonment.

If you are released, you can be rearrested at a later date if the police obtain sufficient evidence and a formal arrest warrant is issued. If a formal warrant is filed within the twenty hours, you will be taken before a judge at the next available opportunity.

Do police have a right to tap my telephone?

Yes. If police can show a judge that they have probable cause to believe that intercepting your telephone conversations is necessary to solve certain crimes, your phone can be tapped by state or federal authorities.

Wiretapping is highly intrusive and it is closely regulated. It will be permitted for only a limited period of time. A less intrusive form of electronic surveillance is a pen register, which records every number dialed from your telephone.

May I represent myself without a lawyer?

Just as you have a constitutional right to the assistance of counsel, you also have the right of self-representation (*pro se*). If you proceed *pro se*, the judge will determine whether you are making a knowing and intelligent decision to give up your right to a lawyer.

The dangers are many. It is not a good idea for untrained people to try to represent themselves in criminal cases. The judge or jury will not necessarily be sympathetic because you have elected to go it alone.

Most people charged with a crime are too close emotionally to their own problems, and they cannot maintain the clear thinking necessary in court. The old saying, "A lawyer who represents himself has a fool for a client," is very true. Self-representation is a large risk that criminal defendants should avoid.

How are criminal charges brought against someone?
There are three ways in which formal charges may be brought: *information*, *indictment*, and *citation*.

An *information* is a written document filed by the prosecutor alleging that the defendant committed a crime.

An *indictment* is a formal charge by a grand jury, a group of citizens convened by the court, in which they determine that there's sufficient evidence to charge a person with a crime and bring him or her to trial. The proceedings are secret.

A *citation* (*summons*) is issued by a police officer, generally for a misdemeanor or minor traffic matter. It is simply an invitation to come to court to answer to charges at a later time.

What is a conspiracy? And what is complicity or accomplice liability?
A conspiracy is an agreement between two or more people to commit a crime, followed by some affirmative activity to carry out the agreement.

The conspiracy itself is a separate crime, even if the crime you were planning was not completed. If you knowingly and affirmatively participated in some manner, then you are an accomplice, aider, or abettor.

If you are a lookout or driving a getaway car, you could be tried for murder during the armed robbery, even if you did not pull the trigger. The theory is that a conspiracy may not have succeeded apart from your contribution, and you can be punished as severely as the other conspirators.

What are plea bargains?

Plea bargains are legal transactions in which a defendant pleads guilty to a lesser charge in exchange for some form of leniency.

The rationale is based on the notion of *judicial economy*. Plea bargains avoid the time and expense of a trial and free the courts to hear other cases. Also, the process is completed much sooner. Defendants are afforded a sense of certainty, knowing generally what the outcome of their case will be rather than taking a chance at trial.

Such offers are often made early in the process and sometimes accompanied with a deadline. If you do not accept the offer, the prosecutor is allowed to withdraw it.

You do not have the right to negotiate a plea as it is within the discretion of the prosecutor. Plea bargains are often made to help reduce heavy caseloads. The judge will probably accept the plea if a legal basis is established in court.

Plea bargaining has become extremely commonplace. Today as many as ninety percent of all criminal cases are settled through plea bargains, although the process is not without its critics.

What kind of evidence may the prosecution use against me at trial?

The prosecution may use almost any type of legally admissible evidence that will help establish your guilt. This includes both physical evidence and testimonial evidence.

The evidence may be direct, such as specific identification of you at the crime scene. It may also be circumstantial or indirect facts showing that you had a motive and committed the crime.

If a witness is asked about someone else's out-of-court statement, it may be objectionable as hearsay, especially if it is being offered for the truth of the matter asserted. The problem with hearsay is that the person who made the statement is not on the stand and is unavailable for cross-examination.

To decide whether the testimony would be hearsay, the court must decide why the witness is being asked the question.

There are many exceptions to the rule against hearsay, so do not be surprised to hear such statements allowed during the trial.

What makes a good witness?

The most important thing is to be honest. When you are on the witness stand, the law requires you tell the truth. Answer questions completely, but stick to the point. Do not volunteer details that are not necessary to answer the question.

If you do not understand the question, politely ask the lawyer to rephrase it. Do not answer questions if you are unsure of the answer. If you don't know, say you don't know.

If you hear a lawyer say, "Objection" after a question is asked, pause and do not answer the question. Wait until the judge rules on the objection.

Testifying can be tiring and frustrating. Remain relaxed and keep a pleasant attitude. The worst thing you can do is appear angry, lose your temper, or argue with a lawyer who is asking the questions. If the jury disapproves of your attitude, they may not believe your testimony.

May the court force me to testify?

If you are a defendant, no. The Fifth Amendment of the U.S. Constitution gives you the right against self-incrimination. If there is any reasonable argument that can be made that your testimony, or any part of it, might incriminate you, then you have the full, complete, and absolute right to refuse to answer on the grounds of the Fifth Amendment.

Do not try to answer some questions and not others, however, because that would be a waiver of your Fifth Amendment rights.

If you are a witness or victim of a crime, a subpoena may be personally served on you. The subpoena compels you to testify, regardless of whether or not you want to get involved.

Sometimes witnesses get cold feet and change their minds about testifying. Although the prosecutor often considers your wishes, technically the case is prosecuted by the state or federal government. Therefore, it is up to the prosecuting attorney to decide whether to proceed with the case and whether to subpoena a witness to testify.

What should I do if I receive a subpoena?

A subpoena is a legal order to appear in court and/or to produce certain evidence.

Be sure to preserve all related documents so that you will not risk being charged with obstruction of justice. Find an attorney and speak to him about the subpoena. Do not confide in friends or contact others who may be in the same situation, since they may be cooperating with the authorities and could end up testifying against you in court.

If you receive a subpoena, you must obey or risk being held in contempt of court.

If it is a *subpoena duces tecum,* you are ordered to produce certain documents. Before obeying this subpoena, call a lawyer. You may wish to contest the subpoena. The lawyer may contact the prosecutor and offer your cooperation, and you may never have to testify. Do not deal with the authorities yourself.

Does discovery take place in criminal cases?

Discovery is a process that allows the parties to learn the strengths and weaknesses of each other's cases, to obtain the names and statements of witnesses the other side intends to call at trial, to identify the nature and location of all physical evidence, and possibly to take depositions.

Answers may be given as long as the question might reasonably lead to the discovery of admissible evidence. Depositions are taken under oath in. a conference room without a judge present.

What is the role of a jury in a criminal case?

The jury weighs the evidence and finds you guilty or not guilty. You have the right to a jury, chosen from a fair cross-section of the community; that is not biased against you.

At the start of the trial, your lawyer will have a chance to voir dire (question informally) the potential jurors.

During the trial, the judge will charge the jury, giving them instructions on how to apply the law to the evidence they have observed at trial.

After the evidence, the jury will deliberate in complete secrecy. If they have questions, they will send a note to the judge, who will normally respond in writing.

If you are found guilty and sentenced by a jury, you will either be fined or given a jail or prison sentence. Don't expect the judge to give you probation or parole, since a judge will normally carry out the wishes of a jury.

Most jury verdicts are the result of a compromise. The verdict must be unanimous, either for guilty or not guilty. If all twelve jurors cannot agree, then a mistrial is declared due to a hung jury and your case is rescheduled for a subsequent trial.

Are there any alternatives to jail or prison?

Yes. One option is monetary, and you may wish to argue that you should be given a fine or made to pay restitution.

Another alternative is counseling, anger control training, psychiatric or psychological therapy, Alcoholics Anonymous programs, etc. These programs should be faithfully attended and completed.

Another option involves community service, where you would be required to donate a certain number of hours to doing service work in the community.

You may also be required to perform certain other special conditions of probation, such as educational or job training classes, serving shock time in the county jail,etc.

May I appeal my conviction?

A person convicted at a trial has the right of appeal. On appeal, you can raise claims of mistakes that were made in applying and interpreting the law. You can claim that the judge erroneously admitted hearsay testimony, gave improper jury instructions, should not have permitted the prosecution to use evidence obtained in violation of your constitutional rights, or permitted the prosecutor to make improper closing arguments.

If the appellate court agrees that there were significant errors in the trial, you could receive a new trial.

DEE
WAMPLER

Republican for

PROSECUTING
ATTORNEY

- 4 years experience in the office as
  YOUR ASSISTANT PROSECUTING ATTORNEY
- Instructor to local law enforcement agencies in criminal law.
- Articles published in two issues of national magazine, "The National Peace Officer"
- Keynote speaker: National Peace Officer's annual Conference - 1970.

DEE, WIFE ANNE, CHILDREN ALLISON AND JOHN are members of King's Way Methodist Church where Dee serves as teacher and Youth Sunday School Superintendent.

Dee's father, Homer, has been a practicing attorney in Greene County for over 30 years.

- **MEMBER** — National District Attorney's Assn., National Peace Officers Assn., Missouri Prosecutors Assn., Missouri Peace Officer's Assn., Greene County, State, American Bar Assn.
- **MEMBER** — Board of Directors, Kiwanis Club.
- **VICE-PRESIDENT** — Civil War Round Table of the Ozarks.
- **GRADUATE** Missouri University Law School (1965), Missouri University (1963). Attended Drury College.
- **U.S. ARMY RESERVE** — 8 years.
- **BORN IN SPRINGFIELD**, attended city schools, active in debate and public speaking at Central and Parkview High Schools.
- **PRACTICING ATTORNEY** in state and federal courts.

In the past four years over 30,000 criminal cases have been handled by this office and Dee has prosecuted almost every kind of felony and misdemeanor case the office handles.

DEE
WAMPLER

REPUBLICAN

FOR

PROSECUTING
ATTORNEY

Dee as elected Greene County Prosecuting Attorney (1967-72)

Starting out as Prosecuting Attorney . . .

To Dee Wampler
Best wishes from
J. Edgar Hoover
6.7.71

FOX NEWS   THE O'REILLY FACTOR
11:22

To order additional copies of

Defending Yourself Against Cops in Missouri

send $24.95 each plus $5.95 S&H* to

Dee Wampler

2974 E. Battlefield

Springfield, MO 6580-4269

or by email: entrapped@aol.com

*add $2.00 S&H for each additional book ordered.

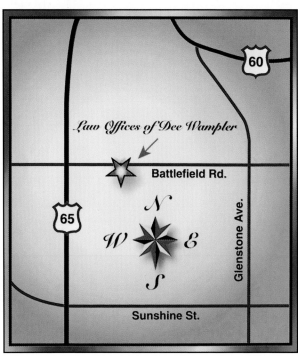

Law Offices of Dee Wampler

Battlefield Rd.

65

60

Glenstone Ave.

N

W   E

S

Sunshine St.

Headshots That Don't Guarantee
The Agent Will Call Back

en Campbell, November 2003

Wynonna Judd, November 2003

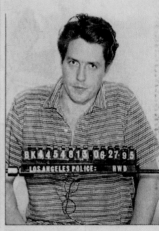

Hugh Grant, June 1995

Santa Barbara County Sheriff's Dept.

11/20/2003
Photo Image of:
NAME: JACKSON, MICHAEL
RAC: B   SEX: M
DOB: 8/29/1958 AGE: 45
HGT: 511   WGT: 120
BLD: CMP:
HAI: BLK   EYE: BRO
MKS:
BOOKING #: 621785

THE CUFFED ONE

Defender of the Accused